Fanshawe's
Indian Summer

Fanshawe's Indian Summer

The Letters of
Lt. Col. Thomas Basil Fanshawe,
33rd (Duke of Wellington's) Regiment

Transcribed by Deirdre Marculescu
Prepared for publication by Derek Alexander

Valence House Publications

Published in 2019 by Valence House Publications
Valence House, Becontree Avenue
Dagenham, Essex RM8 3HT

www.valencehousecollections.co.uk

ISBN 978-1-911391-05-0

Previous Publications
Sebastopol to Dagenham (978-1-911391-02-9)
A History of Dagenham (978-1-911391-03-6)
The Life of Sir Richard Fanshawe (978-1-911391-00-5)
The Death of the 'Dukes' (978-1-911391-99-9)
Abyssinia 1868 (978-1-911391-04-3)
Danger Over Dagenham (978-1-911391-06-7)

Cover Images :
Thomas Basil Fanshawe Portrait - LBBD
Scanned images of TBF letters - LBBD
Regimental Badge
Courtesy of the Duke of Wellington's Regiment Trustees

Thomas Basil Fanshawe (1829 - 1905)

By Mrs Carpenter (1857)

Valence House Museum

Nature's first green to gold,
Her hardest hue to hold.
Her early leaf's a flower;
But only so an hour…

'Nothing Gold Can Stay' – Robert Frost (1874 – 1963)

'You seem to think dearest Mother that I am an evergreen. I am getting on, completed 30 years' service on the 14th on the month and I am getting rather tired of knocking about the world...'

Friday 26th May 1876 – Kamptee, India

Lt. Colonel Thomas Basil Fanshawe was writing to his mother in England from his bungalow at Kamptee in the province of Nagpur, India when he contemplated another solitary weekend ahead.

Through his long career in the 33rd Regiment he had always found lively companions to share his off duty hours. An excellent shot, he enjoyed the quiet camaraderie that came with tracking, hunting and fishing and after, there was the conversation that accompanied those friendships. As a sportsman and natural 'team player' nothing pleased him more than the society of others who shared his interests; but those good times were fast disappearing. Many friends had already retired and others from his younger days had become the casualties of the service. With time on his hands Basil was beginning to regret the passing of those days and wistfully turn his thoughts towards home and family.

Kamptee was a colonial outpost in the established network of camps constantly manned by regiments of soldiers keeping stability in Queen Victoria's Indian colony. The daily routines although robust, were very repetitive and a far cry from the heat of battle at Crimea and Abyssinia, those past high points of Basil Fanshawe's early career.

Basil was in command at Kamptee but if he felt any achievement in gaining that rank he no doubt weighed it against his isolation from other men. Fortunately, his immediate subordinate Major Chadwick was a personable fellow and good company, but he was absent on extended leave and there were only young junior officers currently sharing the mess. Time was passing exceedingly slowly.

Perhaps the relentless heat and the oppressive air contributed to his low spirits, but whatever the cause at that moment, Basil then came to discover he had reached the age to take stock and consider his future. At forty-seven he was ready to admit he missed the comforts of his home in Bath and how difficult he found it to not see his children growing up. With only occasional photographs to monitor their development he sadly reveals his feelings by the intense way he scrutinises their features - *'I do not like Reggy's last photo, the shade on his right cheek or some thing or another makes it look to me swollen & so disfigured it. He seems much grown'.*[1]

Clearly he came to feel it safe to acknowledge to himself that for some time he had known that whilst he was absent overseas, Emily (Minnie), his wife was very unhappy. He had not indulged such thoughts previously for with his practical mind he knew that his chosen career rarely allowed choices and postings away from home and family were part of the job he had signed up for. Only by refusing to think otherwise had he avoided unnecessary personal anguish and his character was such that he would consider it self-indulgent and foolhardy to think differently.

Within these letters we see that as a mature soldier the dominant features of his personality that were revealed in his earlier letters have been maintained. Interestingly we can observe that as soon as he personally was ready to take a re-direction he would explore all possibilities methodically and meticulously. He made certain to identify every option in his approach to problems in his private life;

---

[1] Letter dated September 14th 1876.

that careful approach must have been a useful asset in his professional life too.

Basil's mentor and counsellor throughout his life was undoubtedly his mother Mrs Catherine Fanshawe, the Guernsey born lady who became the wife of the Vicar of Dagenham and owner of the Manor of Parsloes. She wrote continuously to Basil and he valued her opinion above all others. Her calm rationality with the wisdom of life experience is a palpable force weaving through their letters and any information required by Basil was communicated to his mother first.

Seeking her assistance in the question of his possible retirement was vital if Minnie was to avoid stress in the early stages of the plan. Basil's retirement would affect her in many ways; it seems that he was saying to his mother that they must clarify the options, and only when established possibilities were clear would they be presented to his wife to make a final decision together.

Unfortunately for them, in 1876 the best options were not very transparent and complicated by the introduction of new rules and regulations concerning 'purchased' commissions. Changes were being brought in under the Cardwell Reforms which had long been necessary in the modernisation of the vast standing army that kept control over the ever-expanding British Empire.

Having a 'purchased' commission meant that transitional arrangements would apply to Basil and he could not rely on information from previously retired colleagues. His only sources were mainly limited to 'out of date' London newspapers and the confusion of hearsay and rumour that accompanied officers returning from home leave. Not being close to London was obviously a disadvantage as there he could have tapped into his network of connections and reliable contacts built up during his service.

Basil initially needed to keep thoughts about retirement between himself and his Mother and had only the option of communicating his plans in private notes enclosed with his normal letters. He knew it was her practice to pass his letters to others in the family so took the precaution of marking the private notes with instructions that they be burnt. Obviously Mrs Fanshawe ignored his instructions and kept them safe within her collection, this has proved fortunate for us as we may now see how Basil assessed his situation.

His frustration with the poor rates of exchange offered by the government to officers seems understandable, especially as it restricted their capacity to save. Most comprehensible are his feelings concerning any possibility of financial insecurity in retirement - sentiments well recognised by modern day retirees. He ponders too with apprehension the other timeless 'unknowns' - 'will I have enough' and 'how many years must I calculate for my retirement'?

With the benefit of time we know Basil Fanshawe's retirement financial situation was favourable – (see 'Retirement' section). We today also have the advantage of twenty-first century online archival resources and the early twentieth century research of Basil's niece, Mabel Beaujolois Fanshawe and her cousin Herbert Charles Fanshawe[1], - which proves Basil was related to the author of the Cardwell Reforms.

We must assume that Basil did not know his family genealogy in depth, as his father's 3rd cousin Edward Fanshawe was married to

---

[1] The History of the Fanshawe Family, by H. C. Fanshawe (1927) Published by Andrew Reid & Co. Ltd.

Jane Cardwell, a sister of Lord Edward Cardwell. Had he known this connection he might have used the well honoured Fanshawe family network by asking his own older brother, John Gaspard Fanshawe, working in the House of Commons in the service of Cabinet Ministers, to seek first hand advice direct from the newly ennobled Cardwell.

Cardwell had been Gladstone's Secretary of State for War when he drew up the legislation, but before enactment the Liberals were defeated in the election of 1874 by Disraeli's Conservatives. Out of office, Cardwell moved on to the House of Lords but his reforms continued as part of the new government's programme and his name remains attached to the great reforming act.

Basil's lack of knowledge about the wider branches of the Fanshawe family are not surprising as for that generation of the family at Parsloes their social and family relationships were strongest with Mrs Fanshawe's Guernsey families of Le Marchant and Carey. She was the eldest daughter of Major General John Gaspard Le Marchant, the hero of the battle of Salamanca[1] whose illustrious military career and tragic early death came to inspire the young men of succeeding generations to strive to emulate his record. Many achieved senior ranks in various regiments occupying influential positions but during 1876 perhaps the best placed to provide 'insider' information to Basil was Major General Robert Carey. At a later stage in his career, he at that time had an important 'desk job' in Whitehall and a good place to have an ear close to the ground - this gave Basil reason to request his Mother to 'sound him out'.

---

[1] The Battle of Salamanca took place on 22nd July 1812 and was a pivotal victory for Wellington during the Peninsula War. The heroic action of Major General Le Marchant, Commander of the Heavy Brigade resulted in his death on the battlefield but begun the change of events in favour of the British over Napoleon.

This third collection of Basil Fanshawe's letters, written from India, relate to the most mature stage in his army career and readers familiar with his previous letters will know that little interpretation is required. As always he tells his own story well but unlike those from Crimea and Abyssinia there is little action but instead he provides a picture of a life full of routine; common to many other soldiers who served in Britain's colonial India.

The format, style and content are similar to the previous letters but these from India are the most personal for they cover family money matters and are interlinked with familial and national gossip. Obviously they were intended only to be read by his family - those people he loved and even though it is more than a century after his death, we must appreciate how privileged we are to be able to read them.

Writing from Crimea[1], Basil was unmarried and 25 years old, then despatched from India to Abyssinia[2] ten and more years later, we found him married with three very young children and the responsibility of being a senior field officer in his regiment.

Another ten years later, we join him again - a little more world weary as he travels out to India. As always, his personal style is immaculately elegant and his integrity remains constant. Whilst long service and changing situations subdue his youthful spirit he continues to provide an evocative personal account of a period in the history of the British Army which through his eyes can surprise, inform and at times, even disarm.

---

[1] *Sebastopol to Dagenham – The Letters of Captain T B Fanshawe* (Valence House Publications 2016).

[2] *Abyssinia 1868 – The Letter of Major T B Fanshawe* (Valence House Publications 2018).

Fermoy Barracks, County Cork Ireland
Duke of Wellington's Regiment Trustees

NOTE TO COLOURING
BRITISH TERRITORY
HINDU
MUHAMMADAN
British East India Company
INDIA
1857
English Miles
AFGHANISTAN
KASHMIR
Kabul
Jellalabad
Peshawar
PUNJAB
Lahore
Multan
BAHAWALPUR
KUMAUN
NORTH WESTERN PROVINCE
Delhi
Agra
RAJPUTANA
Jeypur
Jodhpur
Ajmir
Gwalior
OUDH
NEPAL
TIBET
SIKKIM
BHUTAN
Darjeeling
Cooch Behar
ASSAM
SIND
Hyderabad
SINDHIA
BEHAR
REWA
Patna
BENGAL
Chandernagore
Calcutta
CUTCH
GUJARAT
MALWA
BHOPAL
Baroda
Indore
Kathiawar
NAGPUR
Nagpur
Sambalpur
Cuttack
BERAR
Aurangabad
Bombay
NIZAM
Hyderabad
ARABIAN
SEA
Goa
Bellary
Cuddapah
MYSORE
Bangalore
Mysore
Madras
COORG
Pondicherry
Laccadive
Islands
COCHIN
TRAVANCORE
Trivandrum
CEYLON
Maldive
Islands
ASSAM
INDEPENDENT
BURMA
Mandalay
Amarapura
LOWER
BURMA
Rangoon
Andaman
Islands
English Miles
Longitude East 80 from Greenwich

Although his viewpoint is first and foremost that of the officer class, his comments and emotions have resonance to the life experiences of so many of all ranks who served in Queen Victoria's Army, many of whom perhaps were our own ancestors. Basil's accounts of their shared journeys and the fascinating sights add colour and texture to historical events that were in the common memory of his time.

Similar to most of the nineteenth century's soldiers with long army service, Basil travelled out to India several times. He served firstly at Dwarka during 1859 when the 33rd Regiment was part of the enforcing troops sent out to India after the Mutiny of 1857. His letters from that experience have not survived but a most excellent graphic account of his and the Regiment's action is given in 'Dying for Glory – The Adventurous Lives of Five Cotswold Brothers'[1]:

'One evening in May 1889 two other officers of the 33rd Foot joined Walter Wynter and Basil Le Marchant[2] for dinner at the (Little Rissington) Manor. Colonel Basil Fanshawe, who commanded the regiment from 1873 until he retired five years later, had served with Wynter throughout the Abyssinian campaign. During his military career Fanshawe also saw action in Crimea and again in 1859 at the siege and occupation of Dwarka, a coastal town some 400 miles north-west of Bombay.

A small expeditionary force, including the 28th Foot (later the 1st Battalion 'The Gloucestershire Regiment'), sailed from Bombay to secure the surrender or capture of a notorious band of Rayput pirates, or Waghurs. Their fort on Beyt Island was attacked and taken, but many of the rebels

---

[1] Michael Boyes – *Dying for Glory – The Adventurous Lives of Five Cotswold Brothers* (Phillimore & Co Ltd 2006).
A fascinating account of the lives and military careers of five sons of Rev. Robert Le Marchant and his wife Eliza Tupper - a niece of Mrs Catherine Fanshawe.
[2] Basil Le Marchant served in the Duke of Wellington's 33rd Regiment from 1881 and retired as Lt. Colonel.

escaped inland. Soldiers looted gold and jewellery from sacred Hindu temples, but orders were later given that the booty be returned.

Meanwhile a smaller force, with Captain Fanshawe second in command, set out from Deesa to reinforce the troops already at Dwarka. Covering 500 miles in 30 days Fanshawe and the men of the 33rd Regiment endured many hardships, frequently wading through flash floods caused by heavy monsoon rains. (Describing conditions during the march Corporal (later Colour Sergeant) John McGrath of the 33rd Regiment wrote 'Scarcely a day past (sic) without our wading through water 3 or 4 times…you can imagine what an unpleasant thing it is to walk or march in wet socks and boots'; later McGrath commented that he and his company went '8 days without taking our boots off').

They arrived just in time to take part in the bombardment of Dwarka, which lasted for 11 days. After the town had been taken sporadic fighting continued for some time in the surrounding jungle, ending with the capture of several hundred Waghur prisoners. Fanshawe and his men remained at Dwarka for three months before marching at a more leisurely pace back to Deesa, their boots in tatters. Much to their consternation those who had taken part in this long-forgotten campaign received no batta (an additional allowance paid to officers and men on campaign in India, perceived by most to be an entitlement), no medal and no share of the prize money available for distribution to other regiments on active service elsewhere in Central India.'[1]

The 33rd Regiment remained at Deesa until late November 1861 and in the absence of any letters we assume that except for periods of

---

[1] Pages 93 and 94 - *Dying for Glory – The Adventurous Lives of Five Cotswold Brothers.*

home leave, Basil Fanshawe's record of service was consistent with the Regimental List of Locations[1].

Records show that the regiment moved to Colaba Barracks in Bombay remaining there until February 1863. Afterwards 'the 33rd' was stationed at Napier Barracks, Kurachee until departing for Abyssinia on 21st November 1867.

During those years overseas Basil would certainly have been home for periods of extended leave. He definitely was in attendance at the Batchelor's Ball in the Assembly Rooms at Bath on 16th April 1863[2] and also on that occasion in those beautifully decorated public rooms was 28 year old Emily Gosselin. She was accompanied by her elder sister Elizabeth and although it is not certain that this was the first opportunity for Basil to meet his future wife, clearly their courtship was soon under way as a formal announcement was made early in January the following year:

'The marriage of Miss Emily Gosselin, the accomplished daughter of G L Gosselin, Esq., of 24 (sic) Park Street, Bath with Captain Basil Fanshawe 33rd Regiment, eldest (sic) son of the Rev T Fanshawe of Parsloes Hall, Essex, is to be solemnised in the month of February next'.[3]

Doubtless Emily's 'accomplishments' were many but perhaps Basil the sportsman was impressed by her talent for archery: *'Weston Archery Club...to compete for two prizes...the first a very elegant gold brooch with turquoises for the greatest number of 'Blues'. – At the close of*

---

[1] Archives of Duke of Wellington's 33rd Regimental Museum, Bankfield Museum, Halifax, West Yorkshire.
[2] The Bath Chronicle & Weekly Gazette 16th April 1863.
[3] The Brighton Gazette 7th January 1864.

the meeting Miss Emily Gosselin was declared the greatest 'Blue' amongst the shooters and the first prize was awarded to her'.[1]

Their marriage took place at Bath on 8th March 1864. Emily was the younger daughter of Gerard Lippeatt Gosselin & Amelia (nee Tupper) originally from Mount Ospringe, Faversham, latterly resident at 28 Park Street, Bath, Somerset. The couple were linked by Guernsey origins and inter-familial marriages over many generations. Their families belonged to the elite and exclusive society on the island which moved within the same circle inevitability leading to families being multi-related. Three of the six children of Basil and Emily also eventually married within those Guernsey families.

After marriage, Basil may not have been in England for the rest of 1864 or Emily may have travelled with him, but in any event by 12th March 1865 she was home in Bath for the birth of their first child, Helen Maude. With these new family responsibilities Basil's career progressed too for within a few weeks he was able to purchase his commission for promotion to the rank of Major in the 33rd Regiment.

Ten years later in these India letters Basil reveals that the purchase was with financial assistance from his older brother John. Through the letters he reveals to his mother that repayment had then become a point of disagreement between them as he states that he was unaware that the money he borrowed in 1865 was actually a debt against Parsloes Manor. He acknowledged he knew the loan must be repaid but was surprised that interest had been added and is particularly unhappy that he has been given short notice to repay the entire debt.

---

[1] Bath Chronicle & Weekly Gazette 10th September 1857.

It is interesting to see Mrs Fanshawe negotiating the problem between her two sons, trying to exercise the 'Wisdom of Solomon' by not favouring one over the other. We have none of her letters but through Basil's remarks we learn that she navigates the dilemma showing that as their mother she would rather pass on her own legacy from her sister than leave her sons to be on bad terms. By being scrupulously fair to each she is successful.

To return once again to Basil's career; after promotion to Major he returned to India during May 1865 accompanied by Emily. Presumably baby Helen was either too delicate or young to withstand the long sea journey around the Cape of South Africa and she remained with Emily's parents in Bath.

Arriving in India Basil and Emily stayed first in the barracks at Kurachee then travelled to the outpost Wanauri Lines at Poona where the following year on 24th April, Emily gave birth to Gerard their second child. Hopefully that little boy helped in some way to compensate for the absence of little Helen Maude but Emily was soon to be kept still more occupied for during December 1866 the family moved back to Kurachee and then on 9th November 1867 another boy, Herbert Cecil was born.

It is easy to imagine how difficult those two years in India must have been for Emily. She had to adjust quickly to marriage, army life, missing her first child and then two further quick pregnancies – and all whilst learning to cope in a foreign land with an exhausting climate. With no family around to support her and no established friendships we can only assume that she was devastated when less than two weeks after the birth of her second son the men of 33rd Regiment were suddenly despatched to the campaign in Abyssinia.

The embarkation of the men was swift leaving Emily to pack up the home and arrange her own and the children's passage back to England. In Basil's letter[1] to Mrs Fanshawe written on 'The Indian Chief' travelling to Annesley Bay he intimates his feelings of helplessness:

With a heavy heart did I leave Minnie & the chicks. She bore up pretty well considering & I do trust that she will have a good journey home. I do not know when I shall hear from her. I have applied for a passage for them on board one of the troop ships that leaves somewhere about the 6th January. Some leave Bombay in the month of December. I hope she will get a passage as it will I expect the same thing to be £150 if they refuse or have too many applications & then have to return by the P & O Steamer. By the troop ship £50 would cover all expenses, that's for herself & Mrs Dunlop[2] who accompanies her home as servant. I trust she will go well but I shall be very glad to know when she is safely settled down at Park Street[3].

It was a sore trial parting & leaving her alone but it could not be helped and the only consolation was that she had got over her trouble while I was there & was going on well. If we had gone when first ordered, this could have been the case'.

In all probability those events caused Emily to be reluctant to repeat the Indian experience and perhaps explain why she was not with Basil when he boarded HMS Jumna for India in November 1875. We cannot be sure and possibly her absence was only because they had four sons and two daughters, with the eldest settled happily into schools in the City. Perhaps too, Mr Gosselin and his wife were growing older, he was nearly 80 and Emily had just too many responsibilities.

---

[1] Letter dated November 27th 1867 *'Abyssinia 1868'*.
[2] Wife of Sergeant John Dunlop, Duke of Wellington's 33rd Regiment.
[3] 28 Park Street, Bath - home of Emily's parents, Mr & Mrs Gerard L Gosselin.

When the regiment returned victorious from Abyssinia on 21st June 1868, it was stationed at Portsmouth Barracks until February 1870. It then transferred to Aldershot and remained until September 1871. Without correspondence or journals we do not know if Basil's wife and children moved with him to any of those locations however, the census taken in the spring of 1871 shows Emily resident with the children at 28 Park Street, Bath living with her parents and sister, but Basil is not there.

Later that year, during September, the 33rd transferred to Colchester remaining two full years. Basil recollects that time spent at Colchester in a letter from India[1]. *'I recollect the Francis's very well – one of the daughters if I mistake not, married a man of the 50th Reg't & was at Colchester with us. Lived a few doors higher up than we did & her brother came down to stay with her. He is a great cricketer & very good Robinson, I think was her husband's name – in the 50th.'* – ('we' could represent his family or the regiment).

Leaving Colchester, Basil and the 33rd moved on to Fermoy in Ireland remaining until April 1875, then transferred to Cork where they embarked for India on 29th October.

Within days, Basil sent news to his mother in London telling her how he was making the best of the situation and aware that he could not change it, was resigned to the prospect of no family life for the foreseeable future. Perhaps the advantage of travel through the Suez Canal, shortening the time at sea by weeks, made his third journey to India more palatable, although he describes the canal as *'more like a big ditch'*.[2]

---

[1] Letter dated October 27th 1876.
[2] Letter dated November 14th 1875.

His letters always reflected his mood and give a curiously mundane account of a period of British India history that is usually seen through a wider lens. They show how the British transported their rigid routines and protocols of English society into that vast land with its own colour and traditions. We learn of the curious obligation maintained at Kamptee to give priority on the arrival of a new commanding officer to paying visits to all the British ladies resident in the area with a bizarre fixed timetable for the visits - as disciplined as any applying to the elegant salons at Bath - *'I have been calling this week on all our married people and as one can only get to a certain number in the regulation hours for paying visits, 12 till 2 – it takes time.'*[1]

As with all Basil's letters he responds to social and familial gossip and Fanshawe family connections to many gentry families over centuries, provide rich material. But times were changing and as the nineteenth century progressed gentlemen of their class needed to find honourable work. A number of Fanshawe men entered the army and navy and progressed well up the ranks but others expanded horizons and entered offices of politics and the colonial services. The more adventurous went on to try their fortunes in the colonies from projects in engineering, mining and later tea and rubber.

Basil Fanshawe was convinced of the important value in honest work and he demonstrates this by his interest and anxiety that all his nephews and younger cousins should make good choices.

He admires those who try entrepreneurial careers and worries with the experience of a senior army officer how base a man's character may be without useful occupation that avoids idleness and

---

[1] Letter dated January 8th 1876.

indulgence : *'I think Joe is very wise in looking out for something to do & not leading an idle life. I wish Ned could find something & Evy. I hope his lady friend Lady Seabright will perform her promise & find him some employment anywhere'*[1].

These letters may contain little exciting action, conflict or battle but their substantial importance lies in the freshness of Basil's accounts of his nineteenth century life. With the background of family activity, we see Victorians making full use of modern transport and communications - staying in touch by frequently travelling with ease, fortunately having reasonable access to money. Details of the celebrations for the Proclamation of the Empress jostle alongside comments on the political scene and the intrigues and gossip surrounding infamous crimes and contemporary mysteries - all varied and interesting topics covered by a lonely officer writing home from the quiet of his 'bungalow'.

Maintaining personal routines was most important to Basil Fanshawe for while he served in India it would reassure his re-entry into the British way of life when he returned home. He reports on his diet and control of the consumption of alcohol, all aided no doubt by his regular fitness regime on the 'racquets' court. Maybe these standards were just typical for his class of officer but in themselves they are indicators of an admirable personal strength of character.

The twenty-first century view of that period of British India, too often sees only the imperial legacy but overlooks the hardship experienced by hundreds of officers and men; the long periods of absence from home, the heat and the tropical diseases, all borne 'for Queen and country'. It is a story owned by many families where

---

[1] Letter dated March 11th 1876.

India is so often not about battle and glory but just as admirably - it tells of fortitude and discipline.

I lost one of my Majors on the 14th of last month. Major Weeding who died from Cholera at a place called Ahmedabad, some hundreds of miles from here in the Bombay Presidency, where he had gone on leave. Taken ill on 12th July & dead on the 14th - one does not get much notice in this country! He was a good officer, but not a man I could make a friend of, poor fellow. I am very sorry & shocked at his end & am afraid it will not calm Minnie's feelings when she hears of it, though so far away from this. It is not a country to live in unless obliged![1]

Despite all Basil Fanshawe's deliberations his decision to retire would not have been easy for his entire adult life had been spent in Duke of Wellington's 33rd Regiment. He knew that the army subdues an individual's character and because of that strict schooling it made the shift into civilian life difficult. His letter of 18th December 1875 tells how he worked on recruits to get them into the 33rd's way: '*I have my hands pretty full as you may imagine with such a lot of men sent to fill up our numbers just as the last moment before leaving Cork. Some of them not even had a Martini Henry rifle in their hands before coming to us, only the old Snider - however, I flatter myself I am working them round by degrees, or rather shall do & it gives me plenty of employment. Not a bad thing in this country.*'[2]

On retirement his own familiar march to the same beat must stop and his habits and routines would need to fit into Park Street, Bath's well-established daily routines. With no rules written down to guide him he knew he must adapt but the security of his careful financial planning sustained him in his confidence in the future.

---

[1] Letter dated August 15th 1876.
[2] Letter dated December 18th 1875.

Sailing toward the Suez Canal on 27th March 1877 Basil's mind was firmly fixed on home and he reported how he tried to make the journey pass more quickly: *'We get thro' the time on board by reading & playing whist at which latter amusement I have been, so far, a winner – a most unusual thing for me as I hold as a rule very bad cards.'*

After that last journey Basil Fanshawe had no need to write long letters and left us without any first hand reports of his life changes. His retirement had lasted almost thirty years when he died in Bath in 1905. Having followed him through his adventures it is difficult not to be curious about the next hand he was dealt.

Editors Comments & Acknowledgements

We have the feeling that Basil is now a 'close friend' and naturally were interested to learn what turns his life took during his remaining years. Research has been rewarding for we soon established that Bath remained Basil's home for the rest of his life and as might have been expected, once he was settled he became extremely active and established himself as a very useful and well respected member of that city's community . In the final section of this book we detail his wide and varied interests which conclude an admirable full life where he offered continued service to others and lived with daily personal enjoyment and fulfilment.

Publishing Basil Fanshawe's letters has been a real delight. We found in his personality so much of interest and many conversation have revolved around each part of the process of bringing his letters to the public. At Valence House we are forever in the debt of John Gordon for providing this unique opportunity of reading, researching and most of all – enjoying his great, great uncle's letters.

John is a son of Strathearn Gordon, grandson of Basil's brother John Gaspard Fanshawe and the letters so lovingly kept by Mrs Katherine

Fanshawe, have become an important part of his family's Fanshawe legacy.

When they were first shown to us at Valence House we realised that they could help expand our knowledge of the nineteenth century family at Dagenham Vicarage and Parsloes Manor. They have never been overlooked but as they were either alive or only recently deceased when 'The History of the Fanshawe Family' was published, their individual stories were unavailable and until now unexplored. Now it is time for them to provide the vital links to the present day Fanshawe family.

For all these possibilities and his continued encouragement we warmly thank John Gordon who gives us special pleasure from his appreciation of our interest and interpretation of the lives of his ancestors through research. John generously donated all of Basil Fanshawe's letter to the Archives & Local Studies Centre, at Valence House Museum, Dagenham and they are now held within The Fanshawe Collection, a vast number of books, papers, documents and family portraits that span five hundred years of Fanshawe family history.

Deirdre Marculescu.
February 2019.

HMS Jumna launched 1866
Harper's Monthly Magazine 1886
Wikicommons

'In these letters from T B Fanshawe almost all the people alluded to by Xtian[1] names are his mother's relations with the exception of his own brothers & sister & their children:

John, Bab – Evy, Bazy, Mabel, Lionel Fanshawe

Helen, Edward – Joe, Nelly, Ned, Charlie, Katie Denison

The Aunts Mary & Caroline are Gostling & Somerville his mother's sisters.

"Fanshawe" whose name appears so often is Mrs Gostling's son, Fanshawe Gostling.

Most of the others are Tuppers – Careys, Le Marchants, Le fervres etc.

"Theodore" being an exception & the son of his father's sister Mrs Boisregan

Miss Faithfull belongs to the elder branch of the family.

"Johnny" is son of Sir Gaspard Le Marchant

The notes on this and the preceding page were prepared by a family member – most probably John Gaspard Fanshawe who held the family collection of papers in his personal library.

---

[1] Christian Names.

Transcribers Notes

Lt.-Colonel Fanshawe's handwriting is relatively easy to read allowing for the semi transparency of the paper. He has written on both sides of each sheet of paper with ink that is not always consistent and he had a need to be economical as postage was prohibitive. As a consequence he made hardly any attempt to punctuate or paragraph his letters to allow more space.

Lack of punctuation creates a problem with the flow of the letters, when read in the original and an early decision was made to insert punctuation in the transcription for ease and enjoyment of the letters.

No other 'improvements' were necessary, as his spelling was almost perfect and he made very few errors that were not self-corrected. As with all good correspondents he wrote with energy and immediacy.

With patience I have transcribed most of his words, but those that elude me are shown by the symbols below.

[ ]   transcribers addition or comment.
[xxx]   indecipherable word or part word - x relating
               to approximate number of letters.
( )   comments bracketed by TBF in his letters.

Place Names - mostly verified by maps, but within the letters TBF occasionally uses various different spellings for the same place.

Letter from Thomas Basil Fanshawe to his mother Mrs Catherine
Fanshawe
H.M.S. Jumna[1]
Sunday November 14th (1875)

My dearest Mother,

I wrote to John[2] from Malta[3], or rather posted my letter from there
and he no doubt will have told you how we got on after leaving
Queenstown[4]. We have had the most enjoyable weather since Malta,
smooth sea, bright sun with just breeze enough to prevent us feeling
it too much.

We got to Port Said[5] this morning, about 8 and left about 12. It is
now about 2 and we are in the canal[6] about 12 miles from Port Said
and it is most uninteresting, it is more like a big ditch. We have seen

---

[1] H.M.S. Jumna, a rigged steamer built by Palmers Shipbuilding & Iron Co,
launched in 1866. One of five ships commissioned to transport troops via the Suez
Canal it could travel at 15 knots and had the capacity to accommodate a battalion of
infantry.

[2] John Gaspard Fanshawe (1824 – 1903), elder brother of TBF and owner of Parsloes,
Dagenham.

[3] Malta became part of the British Empire in 1800 and provided the British army
and navy with a strategic position in the Mediterranean - particularly after the Suez
Canal opened in 1869.

[4] Queenstown, a seaport on the southern coast of County Cork, Ireland, historically
linked to mass migration to U.S.A during the nineteenth century and also
embarkation of British troops to the Indian continent.

[5] On the N.E. Mediterranean coast of Egypt, Port Said was established in 1859 as a
consequence of the construction of the Suez Canal - it lies about 30 kilometres from
the canal entrance.

[6] Connecting the Mediterranean Sea to the Red Sea, the Suez Canal was constructed
within 10 years and opened in 1869 when it reduced by weeks the journey from
Europe to the Indian Ocean. The canal with a single lane and without locks, is
maintained and owned by the Suez Canal Authority and protected by the
Convention of Constantinople, so that it remains open in time of war or peace for
the use of every vessel of commerce or war, without distinction of flag.

heaps of ducks and flamingos[1] – the only thing to divert ones attention.

I got no letters at Malta from anyone as the mail had not come in before we left, but I got two this morning, one from 33 and the other from 28 Park Street. Minnie's[2] written in rather better spirits I think, dated 4th Nov. & Mr [or Mrs] Gosselin[3] gave me a pretty fair account of the Le Marchants[4].

I found Malta very hot - I suppose after being used to the sea breeze on land.

I had a paper sent me containing the result of the Royal Commission[5] if true, which Minnie seems to conclude as it has been put forward as a feeler, it will not benefit me in the least and utterly ruin Chadwick[6] as it will prevent him ever getting command.

I am glad to hear that Aunt Caroline[7] was better, so I trust you will not have to make a journey there again. Tell Helen[1] please with my

---

[1]Lesser Flamingos – tall wading birds with distinctive pink plumage are found in the Sub Sahara regions of Africa, across the Arabian Peninsula and also in India & Pakistan.

[2] TBF's wife – Emily Catherine Gosselin (1835 - 1926).

[3] Gerard L Gosselin & Mrs Amelia Gosselin were the parents of Minnie. Descendants of ancient Jersey & Guernsey families, they resided at Bath.

[4] Catherine Le Marchant, TBF's mother was in close contact with her nine surviving brothers & sisters and their children. Numerous references to the Le Marchant family of Guernsey are contained in the letters of TBF.

[5] The Royal Commission on Officers' Grievances.

[6] Lieutenant-Colonel Edward Frederick Chadwick - born 3rd March, 1829, enlisted as an Ensign in 59th Regiment. Promoted to Major in 1866 & Lieutenant-Colonel 1875. He transferred to 33rd (Duke of Wellington's) Regiment. He retired in 1878 with the rank of Colonel on full pay. Formerly of Chesnole and later Westfield, Dorchester, he married Amy, daughter of Revd. Charles Torkington and Ellen Cookson in 1882.

[7] Caroline Le Marchant Somerville (b1802), sister of TBF's mother and widow of Captain John Somerville (1796 – 1852) Royal Artillery, lived at Heavitree, near Exeter in Devonshire.

Suez Canal
Egypt State Information Service

Narrow gauge engine on the road to Kamptee circa 1880
The Indian Railways Fan Club

love, that the glasses have been most useful and capital good ones I have found them, & the watch keeps first rate time.

Have you heard again from Dick[2]? I hope the new girl in Caroline's place will suit.

Corporal Derby, Derby's husband had made up his mind to purchase his discharge. I hope it will not be the cause of Minnie losing Mrs Derby.

We expect to be at Suez tomorrow afternoon if all goes right, and I suppose it will be another fortnight before we reach Bombay[3]. I shall not be sorry when I get the Regt comfortably settled at Kamptee[4] and see how I shall like the place. The dress bugle[5] for dinner, 4 o'clock is just going, so I will bring this dull scrawl to an end, keeping it open till tomorrow, in case I may have anything worth jotting down.

With best love to Helen, John and belongings & self

Ever dearest Mother, your most affectionate son

Basil

---

[1] Helen Denison - widow of Edward Hanson Denison (died 1864), only surviving sister of TBF.
[2] Richard Fanshawe - younger brother of TBF.
[3] Bombay (Mumbai from 1995) situated on the west coast of India had historical interest for TBF as his ancestor, Sir Richard Fanshawe had negotiated the marriage contract on behalf of King Charles II and Catherine of Braganza, the Portuguese Princess, whose dowry included control of the city of Bombay.
[4] Kamptee - originally Camp-T (due to the shape), set up as a military base by the British army in 1821 and situated on the Kanhan River in the district of Nagpur.
[5] Bugle calls, traditionally used by armed forces of many countries were highly effective in conveying messages or commands over long distances. Modern communications have replaced bugle calls except for ceremonial occasions and at military academies and training centres.

Letter from Thomas Basil Fanshawe to his mother
Kamptee
Dec. 18th (1875)

My dearest Mother,

I have to thank you for your last of Nov. 18th which reached me this day week & very glad I was to get it & hear how you all were getting on.

I wrote to Helen last week and asked her to tell you of having safely reached this place without any contretemps barring the baggage being knocked about a good deal.

I have my hands pretty full as you may imagine with such a lot of men sent to fill up our numbers just as the last moment before leaving Cork. Some of them not even had a Martini Henry rifle[1] in their hands before coming to us, only the old Snider[2] - however, I flatter myself I am working them round by degrees, or rather shall do & it gives me plenty of employment. Not a bad thing in this country.

This is a very pretty canton[3], nice & nicely kept, the people very civil – they put up the whole of our married ladies so they could settle down in bungalows[4] of their own. Chadwick & I went to live with

---

[1] Martini–Henry rifles came into use in the British Army during 1871 and remained the standard service rifle for 20 years. They were tilt-block single-shot breech-loading and operated by a lever beneath the wrist of the buttstock.

[2] The .577 Snider–Enfield was a breech-loading rifle brought into use in the British Army in 1866. The firearm action was invented by Jacob Snider, an American and incorporated into the Snider–Enfield rifle, replacing the Pattern 1853 Enfield muzzle-loading rifle.

[3] A territorial or administrative subdivision in India.

[4] Derived from the Gujarati word 'bangalo' meaning Bengali as this design of house came from the Bengal area of South Asia. The original bungalows were small, single storey, detached and with a verandah.

the General. Walker[1] whom I knew many years ago at Kensal Moor[2] Manchester in the 30th regiment, we were both subs together[3]. He is much liked here.

Chadwick & self, have got a very comfortable bungalow, in fact one of the best in the lines and close to the mess which is a great advantage, particularly in the rains and we are settling down by degrees. I have been lucky in having had a horse lent me by a Colonel Dance[4] of the Artillery who is going away on six months home & who kindly made the offer that if I liked to keep the horse, I might. Too good a thing to be refused as horses are very hard to get in these parts. In fact none are in the market.

Chadwick is going on duty up to Delhi[5], only just 11 hundred miles from here by sail, for the camp of exercise there and he and I both trust that after the camp is over, that he will be able to pick up a decent animal for each of us.

The climate just now is charming; morning & evening it is quite cold, though we don't have frost – the sun has power even now. I

---

[1] General Sir Mark Walker VC, KCB (1827 – 1902) of the 30th Regiment - awarded the VC at the Battle of Inkerman in Crimea *'jumped over a wall in the face of two battalions of Russian Infantry which were marching towards it. This act was to encourage the men, by example, to advance against such odds – which they did and succeeded in driving back both battalions'*.

[2] Kensal Moor was a large open heath area close to Salford, Manchester that was used by the military for displays and inspections. During 1838 it had also been the site for one of the largest demonstrations by the Chartists.

[3] Probably 1848, when the 33rd was stationed at Manchester.

[4] Colonel Edward William Dance, Royal Artillery.

[5] Delhi came under the control of the British Government following the end of the Indian Rebellion of 1857 and was a district province of the Punjab. In 1911 the status of capital was transferred to Delhi from Bombay (Mumbai).

fancy this place very much, like Deesa[1] as to heat in the daytime & everyone says that it is <u>hot</u>!!! in April, May & June, but the rains seem to be the part of the year most disliked, being hot & steamy.

There are only one or two proud & happy possessors of carriages & horses in this place, a covered cart drawing trotting bullocks is the most approved mode of conveyance – you get over the ground about six miles an hour.

I & Chadwick have been fully occupied all the week in calling on all the ladies of the station, it being the correct thing to do as a newcomer – we finished the job yesterday, you can only call between 12 & 2 and as one has some distance to go one cannot accomplish many in a day. There is not much beauty in the place & I am sorry to say that except big game shooting (tigers[2], bison[3] & sambar[4]) - in the hot weather, there is none. 4 of our people went out for a couple of days this last week & returned empty handed – though they saw some antelope[5] & Bustard[6]. So I do not think there is much inducement to go out. It is just a sell[7], for I had heard that it was such a capital place for shooting.

---

[1] The 33rd Regiment served at Camp Deesa which had been set up in 1820 to secure and resist incursions from the desert regions. The town of Deesa sits on the eastern bank of the River Banas.

[2] Currently, India has 70% of the world's population of tigers.

[3] Indian bison called Gaur, native to South Asia & Indian subcontinent are massive bovines - the largest and tallest of the species.

[4] Sambar, the large deer, native to the Indian subcontinent also found in southern China and South East Asia.

[5] Antelope, similar to deer have smooth coats of fur and pointed ears. They are courageous and fast running and are found across Africa & Asia.

[6] The great Indian bustard is a large ground bird about 3 foot tall found across India in dry arid land. Their numbers are at risk today.

[7] A misleading trick or a swindle.

I believe the big game shooting <u>is</u> good - & the pig sticking[1] but as I cannot ride a lent horse at that game it does not make much difference to me. There is though some good Mahseer[2] fishing to be had some little way off which I mean to have a try at when I have a little more time on my hands.

 I have been quite well since I left England except a bit seedy the day we left the ship, which I think was caused by the sun the previous afternoon as I was weak enough to only wear a forage cap[3] on board deck thinking the awning overhead was enough protection, however I was all right again at night.

I have two good servants as times go at least, I have not yet discovered their own peculiar iniquities at present.

I am very glad when the clock keeps good time in the dining room but it was only a trifle after all your goodness to us. I am very sorry to find that Evy[4] can find nothing to do – it must be very bad for him and with so many temptations in London & time is getting on over his head & what he would accept as a young man, as he gets older he will think beneath his dignity to accept.

---

[1] Pig Sticking involved chasing wild hog or pigs whilst on horseback and catching them with a spear. Prior to the British army in India, the natives of the area hunted wild hogs by foot but the British Army officers turned it into a sport using horses and a longer lance. Open and closed seasons were operated and the sport was shared with the Maharajas. Notably, in 1889 Capt. Robert Baden Powell, (Lord Baden-Powell, founder of Scouting & Guiding Associations) published a manual *'Pigsticking & Hoghunting'*.

[2] Golden Mahseer, the largest fish of the species and found up to 9 foot long and weighing over 100 lbs. First described in 1822 by Francis Buchanan-Hamilton, once British anglers arrived in India these fish became highly sought after.

[3] The regimental peaked cap with a woollen cover designed for use whilst foraging.

[4] Evelyn J Fanshawe (1854-1949) – nephew of TBF, eldest son of John Gaspard Fanshawe of Parsloes.

I should think John was rather pleased than otherwise at not retiring from his office[1] – particularly if he lost money by so doing.

Seymour Le Marchant[2] is evidently doing no good by his stay in Guernsey – what a pity he should commence life so badly & waste his existence in the way he is doing. What does Johnny[3] do and where is he living now? Have the family come to any agreement as to the terms of the will[4] of their father?

I shall be very grateful for any information that Robert Carey[5] can pick up about the labours of the Royal Commission, if the feeler that appeared is true or partly so, it would not (the scheme) benefit me in the slightest degree & no rank in the army seems at all satisfied with what is proposed.

I shall give you no news from Bath as no doubt Minnie keeps you well informed of her & the chicks' doings. The boys I presume, are having their Xmas holidays – I am glad they still liked going to school[6] & that, after the novelty had worn off.

Not much like Xmas weather this – every door & window open and dressed in lighter clothes than we would wear in the hottest day at

---

[1] John G Fanshawe retired from his position at the Board of Trade in the year following this letter. He was Private Secretary to Cabinet Ministers - Lord Stanley, the Duke of Richmond and Mr T Milner Gibson.

[2] Seymour Le Marchant (1854 – 1924) 1st cousin of TBF - born in Halifax Nova Scotia, son of Sir John Gaspard Le Marchant GCMG KCB (1803–1874) Lt. Governor of Nova Scotia (1852–1858).

[3] John Gaspard Le Marchant (born 1843) – older brother of Seymour Le Marchant.

[4] Probate granted to widow, Margaret Anne Le Marchant (under £14000) following Sir John Gaspard le Marchant's death in 1874.

[5] Robert Carey (1821–1883) a relative via paternal grandparents was married to Caroline Le Marchant a 1st cousin to TBF. With a distinguished military career, in particular during the New Zealand wars of 1860-1866, he retired with the rank of Major General. In the period 1870–1882, he was Deputy Judge Advocate at Army HQ in London.

[6] Bath School, 20 Portland Place, Bath.

Major General Robert Carey
Deputy Judge Advocate at HQ (1870 - 82)
History of the Carey Family of Guernsey (careyroots.com)

British Tommies of the Army Service Corps
and the Royal East Kent Regiment
Working on a regimental soda machine circa WW1
Royal East Kent Regiment

home in summer & the hot sun enough in the day to make an umbrella very pleasant over one's head.

We have a capital mess house & a decent mess man. We are getting our billiard[1] table out, which will be a comfort. Our regimental [printing] press is at work & we are busy in trying to get our regimental soda water making[2]

machine to work but some part was damaged on route. The price of carriage by sail is very great, the cost of carriage of billiard table from Bombay to here was over £20 & they have just issued the duty on wines at the customs house at Bombay. So what with that, the carriage up & carriage out from home, wine will be an expensive article – I fancy the sherry will be something like 5/6[3] or 6/- a bottle, champagne 10/- or 12/- a bottle.

I stick to my cup of cold tea at night instead of spirits as much as I can, though I sometimes take a soda & brandy in the middle of the day & trust it does one good now & then. As I cannot drink beer though I should like to, & a bottle of claret is too much at one time & does not improve by being open, it is hard to know what to drink but most days I go from breakfast to dinner without touching anything.

---

[1] Billiards date from at least the fourteenth century and have been mentioned by Shakespeare & Dickens and many other writers. In 1875, the English Billiard table would probably be at least 6 feet long and the game played with two cue balls and a red object ball. The aim of scoring either a fixed number of points, or the most points within a set time frame was agreed by the players beforehand.

[2] In the eighteenth century Joseph Priestley invented a machine to aerate water by introducing carbon dioxide into water and by 1850 carbonated drinks were being commercially manufactured and in Barking at the R. White Lemonade factory. In tropical India a soda water machine would be invaluable not only for a variety of flavoured drinks but also to produce tonic water with the additional ingredient of quinine to serve as a prophylactic against malaria.

[3] 5/6 - represents five shillings & sixpence (pre 1971 British Currency).

I was up at 7 this morning for office work, no parade on Saturdays & being mail day I found several ~~hundred~~ bundles of letters. 2 or 3 hundred which I had to frank for the men to go for a journey to England. I first had time to come back & dress & then see the men's bks [barracks] & kits which took me to 12 & at 12.30 I got breakfast.

We shall not get our letters of November 25th till Monday I am afraid, as the steamer was only signalled at 5.30 this morning coming into Bombay. Receiving letters is one of the greatest pleasures out here, at least it is to me.

How I have been scribbling on, you will be quite glad to come to an end.

So wishing you all in London & yourself in particular, all the best wishes of the season, though I am afraid I am rather late or rather will be when this arrives. With best love, ever dearest mother,

Your most affectionate son

Basil

Letter from Thomas Basil Fanshawe to his mother
Kamptee
Saturday January 8th (1876)

My Dearest Mother,

Many thanks for your last of Dec. 12th which reached me yesterday. I suppose you will have just received mine, I wrote from here about 18th of last month.

I do not dislike this place but fancy it is very hot in the hot weather, very like Deesa I imagine but with this drawback, that there is no shooting to be got from here, as there was at Deesa. Several of our people have been out but done very little & unless one makes a regular job of it & get leave & go away some 60 or 100 miles, it is not worth going out for.

Our climate just now is pleasant enough, the mornings & evenings are quite cold & one can stand a blanket on one's bed very comfortably – I am pretty well settled down & have got a horse bought via an Arab which belonged to a Colonel of the Artillery who was leaving the place and as it is a good horse I think myself lucky to get one for the price I did - £80.

There has been a good deal going on one way or another, the General had a large dinner party of 22 on Xmas Day to which I went. A very good dinner! He gave a ball on New Year's night. Asked for nine o'clock & so I thought if I went at 10 it would be time enough but I found all the ladies had their cards[1] full, so I thought it very slow & got away about 12, though I hear they kept it up till past three.

---

[1] Small decorative booklets listing the programme of dances at a formal ball. Usually attached to the lady's wrist, they were available to record the names of gentlemen to whom a promise had been made for a particular dance.

The General looked at us on parade last Monday & he told me afterwards that he had reported the Reg't unfit for service on account of the boys we have in the ranks. He is quite right, I do not believe they could march 10 miles in this country with their full accoutrements on. I have sent 40 men away to a hill station called Pachmarhi[1] & I have no doubt I shall send a lot home before long. One can never get a good regiment nowadays with this six years' service[2], for as soon as the men are really soldiers and worth anything they take their discharge. However, I suppose it will last my time!

I have been quite well since I have been out here, lots to do one way & another. I take plenty of exercise, up at 6 every morning – parade & riding room work & I seldom get breakfast before 10.30 & I find I can go very well till dinner without touching anything.

I usually play racquets[3] from 4 to 5.30 & indulge sometimes in a brandy & soda after, the only spirits I touch & stick to my cup of cold tea at night before going to bed.

I have been calling this week on all our married people and as one can only get to a certain number in the regulation hours for paying

---

[1] Pachmarhi was a hill station in Madhya Pradesh state of central India widely known as Satpura ki Rani "Queen of Satpura" situated at a height of 1100m in a valley of the Satpura Range in Hoshungabad.

[2] The Army Enlistment Act of 1870 initiated by Cardwell, reduced normal service from 21 years to 12 years. It also provided that soldiers would usually only serve 6 years and the remaining years would be spent on the reserve list. This aimed for greater flexibility to increase or reduce the Army with ready trained men, as and when the need arose.

[3] Racquets is played either as singles or doubles within an enclosed court 30' x 60' and using a 'bat' & hard ball, strokes must touch the walls. The game was kept in play with the ball hitting the ground only once. It is a fast and potentially risky game which evolved during eighteenth century when there was limited space for activity in the prisons of the Fleet and the King's Bench. During the nineteenth century it was most often played at public schools.

Pachmarhi hill station
Wikicommons

Sir Arthur Upton Fanshawe
LBBD Archives at Valence House

visits, 12 till 2 – it takes time. And I have been on a board inspecting all the arms of the Reg't as well this week. So I have not much spare time…

I hear from Minnie regularly, she has not yet heard of my arrival in Bombay but will ere this. I shall not give you any Bath news as you get it first hand – my friend Chadwick has gone away to Delhi for the camp of exercise there and I cannot expect him back before middle of next month, so I am all alone in my bungalow. However, I am not in it much, except to write letters. Arthur Fanshawe[1], a cousin or connection is in the civil service at Nagpur 10 miles from here. I like what I have seen of him, he lent me a horse to ride in on arrival. He came & slept in my house the other night as he was dining with the Artillery. I did not see much of him, as he came just before 7 o'clock in time to dress & left at 8 the following morning. He has promised to come & dine soon, he has a wife & 2 children whom I suppose I must call on. I hear she is nice.

What a difference there is between our climate & yours! The thermometer here goes up to 136° in the <u>shade</u>!!! – in the hot weather, so you will have the best of it then.

I am glad to find that you did not hurt yourself when you fell in Eaton Square. I wish I had been there to pick you up. Lizzie[2] had a fall in Bath & luckily did not hurt herself. She always does come to grief if it is possible to do so.

---

[1] Sir Arthur Upton Fanshawe, K.C.E.I., C.V.O (1848 - 1931) was a distant cousin of TBF via the Dengie branch of the Fanshawe family. He arrived at the HQ station at Hoshungabad in 1871 and in 1873 married Louisa Chase, daughter of a captain in the Bengal Army. He advanced in the Colonial Service and at retirement held the establishment appointment in Bombay of Director-General of the Post Office in India.

[2] Elizabeth Caroline Gosselin (1831 - 1905) - unmarried elder sister of Emily, TBF's wife.

I am pleased to hear you have heard again or rather John heard from Dick & that he liked the things he had received. I wish his leg would get well & he got a turn of luck somehow & got a start, everything seems to go wrong – I hope John & Bab's[1] colds are well – what a pity Evy does not do something. Your account of Seymour Le Mat is not a flourishing one. Johnny le Mat seems to cho[o]se his wives[2] from a much lower grade in life than he would have done had he remained in the army – or his father would have approved of.

[I] am sorry to hear Blanche[3] is under the doctor's care. Aunt Caroline seems no worse, how does she like the cold weather you have been having?

We have been having a lot of big dinners & have more in prospect returning the hospitality we accrued on arrival. Rather late you will say but all our silver centre accoutrements went astray & we had to wait their recovery. We had a small party of 34 last Tuesday including the General – a very good dinner. But was most unfortunate in not getting ice from Bombay which we had ordered. We have the Artillery to dine with us next Tuesday and then 35th Reg't Native Infantry[4] & others after that. Our troops here are comprised in ourselves, two field batteries of Artillery, the 35th Reg't, the 7th & a wing of the 22nd Reg't., Native Infantry. I shall be glad when these big dinners are over as I do not care about them & I am kept up later than I like, with having to be up early in the morning.

---

[1] Barbara Fanshawe, née Coventry (1832 - 1903) – TBF's elder brother's wife.
[2] Married Jane Finch 1875 at St George, Hanover Square when J G Le Marchant was described on the certificate as a 'bachelor'.
[3] Blanche le Marchant (1868 – 1931) one of nine daughters of Revd. Robert Le Marchant, Rector of Little Rissington & his wife Eliza Tupper (1st cousin of TBF).
[4] Bengal Native Infantry regiments – former East India Company regiments were not finally absorbed into the British Indian Army until 1903.

I am afraid I have written a most disjointed production but I have had constant interruptions of different sorts. Am glad you give good accounts of the Russells[1], give her my love when you see her – any chance of either of the girls changing their names?[2] I wrote to Helen from this & John from Bombay. It seems to me, much longer than two months & a half since we left Cork. I must bring this to an end for here is the Postman come for letters & if I do not post it today it will make a week's delay in your receiving it. Our mail are not very regular in arriving. They ought to be in Bombay early in the week & we should then get the letters on a Friday, it being a two days post. Last week we had no English mail, this week had one on Monday & the other yesterday.

Now goodbye dearest Mother & with much love to you and all in Halkin Street[3] & Wilton Place[4].

Ever you most affectionate son

Basil

---

[1] Family of Champion Branfill Russell living at Stubbers, North Ockendon, Essex.
[2] By marriage.
[3] 2 Halkin Street West – London address of John Gaspard Fanshawe.
[4] Wilton Place, Hanover Square – London address of Helen Denison.

Letter from Thomas Basil Fanshawe to his mother
Kamptee
February 5th (1876)

My Dearest Mother,

Many thanks for your last of January 13th which reached me yesterday, Friday morning - but am very sorry to hear your account of Aunt Caroline & that there is little or no hope of her moving. It must be a trying time for you and I do not think you ought to be all alone with her in the state she is in but at this distance it is no use my suggesting anything for they would arrive far too late.

You must have had a very cold journey down, am glad you had a peep at May[1] & Gerry[2] at the station on your way – the former sent me her photo, a new one, the other day, she seems to be a good deal grown or perhaps her winter dress makes her appear so. I thought the report of Mrs Andrews[3] on the boys, was very good. I only hope they will keep it up in future.

In future should any bills arrive for me at 15 Gloucester Street[4], or letters that I asked you to open, I think if you would send them to Minnie it would be best. Would you kindly send her that little bill of Hollands[5] you mentioned as having received?

---

[1] TBF's eldest child, Helen Maude Fanshawe born at Bath 12 March 1865 – died June 1950.
[2] TBF's eldest son Gerard Lewis Fanshawe – born in India 24 April 1866. Enlisted in the Corps of Engineers and promoted to Major 1902, died in Malta during 1904 due to 'Maltese Fever' aged only 38.
[3] Mrs Jane Andrews and her husband George were joint principals of Bath School at 20 Portland Place, Bath (1871 Census).
[4] 15 Gloucester Street – London home of Mrs Catherine Fanshawe.
[5] Possibly Messrs Holland & Sons, of Marylebone Road, London, the nineteenth century cabinet makers with a Royal Warrant.

I heard from her & Mrs Gosselin, the 4 eldest children had been the night before she wrote, to a fancy dress ball & the two girls looked very well. But I had better gossip about myself than give you what in most likely a 2nd edition at a very old tale.

We are gradually getting into the grooves of the place. We have had some unusually hot weather in the daytime for the time of year, but it has been cooler the last 10 days. The nights, mornings & evenings are still cool & pleasant though. I have had no shooting, nor shall I this season as you must go for a very long way for anything good & as we are inspected this month, on or about 20 or 21st - I have plenty to keep me here.

I was asked to go & fish by a man yesterday - towards the end of the month, which I should much like to do, but I am afraid I could not manage it. The fish is called Mahseer – sometimes runs to a good size, 20 to 40 lbs not uncommon, & they have been caught larger. I am told they are capital eating, see how opinions differ. Perhaps I may be able to give you my own on the subject. Tell John I have got some bustard[1] feathers for him & think I have a chance of sending them home next week. One of our fellows shot a bustard last week & sent me the bird as a present, it weighed 15lbs after plucking all the valuable feathers. I sent the carcase to a Mrs Fenn[2] of ours, as it is capital eating – and she told me it was very good indeed.

I am glad to say Chadwick came back from the Delhi trip on Thursday, half an hour before his letter to me arrived – and I am not sorry to have him back.

---

[1] Bustard – a bird extinct in UK from 1830. Early this century a similar species was successfully re-introduced from Russia.
[2] Wife of Captain Edwin Glass Fenn (33rd Regiment) - enlisted as an ensign 1859.

Last night at Nagpore[1] 10 miles off, there were some private theatricals & a dance. I am thankful to say I was not honoured with an invitation, though Arthur Fanshawe's wife wrote & asked me to sleep & stay at their home if I was going. I must try & get over there some day & make her acquaintance. I feel quite ashamed of myself not having done so.

Next week there are some races here but I fancy they are not much, very few horses to run or people to attend. Just now a native festival called the Moharram[2] is going on & the row from the bazaar of the native drums called Tom Toms[3] is great & very wearisome. Pray excuse this blot [*smeared ink on the original letter*] – I did not see it on the paper when I began & have not time to rewrite – or shall lose the post.

I have been out twice to dinner since I wrote last, very good dinners but rather slow afterwards & we have been giving Regt'l dinners to people who have called on the mess & returning those given to us. I am truly thankful to say we have polished the whole lot off & have no more in prospect. I have been sticking pretty close to parades & racquets in afternoon, I find I get more exercise at that amusement than in any other way.

---

[1] Nagpur Province (called by the British, Nagpore) came under the administration of a commissioner of the British central government, with Nagpur as its capital. After the arrival of the Great Indian Peninsula Railway (GIP) in 1867 the area developed as a trade centre.

[2] Moharram - commemorates the martyrdom of Imam Hussain, the grandson of Prophet Mohammed, observed by Muslims throughout India with impressive processions of colourfully decorated Tazias, (paper and bamboo replicas of the Martyr's tomb at Karbala).

[3] A tom-tom drum is a cylindrical drum with no snares – Anglo-Indian the name originates from the Sinhala language.

Am glad to hear that Bazy[1] has gone back to Erith[2], wish you had been able to tell me that Evy had something to do – how is Helen & Katie[3]? I wrote to John the mail before last so you will no doubt have heard of my doings.

Edward Le Marchant[4], 67th wrote to me the other day from Rangoon[5] where he had just arrived from up country preparatory to coming to this Presidency. I met one of his brother officers last night who gave a very good opinion of him & said he was a great favourite in the Reg't. How is his mother? The cold weather you are having must be rather trying to her, I should think. Minnie writes how she does not like it at all – Mr Gosselin says he is suffering from rheumatism in his knee, & Mrs G from a cold which she cannot get rid of. Lizzy seems to be very flourishing. Minnie says Liz & her Father do nothing but go out to Kettledrums.[6]

I wonder when the result of the Royal Commission on the Officers will be made public? I am afraid from all accounts every rank will be

---

[1] Basil Fanshawe, (engineering apprentice), nephew of TBF 2nd son of John Gaspard Fanshawe.

[2] South of the River Thames, Erith was a centre for engineering where during the winter 1875/6 a long union backed strike disputed changes in day to piece working.

[3] Helen & Katherine Denison - aged 30 and 12 were daughters of Edward & Helen Hansen Denison - nieces of TBF.

[4] Edward Henry Le Marchant (Born 1853), Hampshire Regiment - son of TBF's 1st cousin Eliza Tupper & Revd Robert Le Marchant of Little Rissington – attained the rank of Lt. Colonel but at a regimental gymkhana on 23rd May 1899 was shot dead by an assassin who was captured, tried and hung. Le Marchant is buried at Taikal, Peshawar.

[5] Rangoon or Yangon, seized by the British in the 2nd Anglo-Burmese War of 1852 was transformed into the commercial and political hub of British Burma. It was based on the design of army engineer Lt. Alexander Fraser on a grid plan, on delta land, bounded by the Pazundaung Creek and the Yangon River. After the Indian Rebellion of 1857, the last Mughal emperor Bahadur Shah II, was sent to live in Rangoon.

[6] Informal social parties held in the afternoon or early evening where guest would be served with a light collation (light informal meal).

sold – not get anything like what they anticipated, however I do not think it will make much difference in my plans, in inducing me to go any sooner or later.

I hear we are to have a draft of 100 men to come out, they were to leave about 20th this month. We were at least that under our strength when we left Cork.

Here comes the man for letters, so I will shut up what I am afraid is a very stupid production – so with best love to all in Halkin Street & Wilton Place – has Ned[1] got anything to do yet? I suppose Charlie's[2] Reg't will be coming out this year or early next. I wonder if he will like this country, if he comes to it?

Ever dearest Mother

Your most affectionate son

Basil

---

[1] Edward Fanshawe Denison (1849 – 1899) 2nd son of Helen Denison & nephew of TBF.

[2] Albert 'Charles' Denison (1852-1896) 3rd son of Helen Denison and a nephew of TBF. Lt. in the 100th (Prince of Wales's Royal Canadian) Regiment of Foot.

Letter from Thomas Basil Fanshawe to his mother
Kamptee
Saturday March 11th (1876)

My Dearest Mother,

Your last of February 18th reached me this morning. Many thanks for such a long one, though sorry to find you had so much on your hands. How glad you must be to feel that you have nearly come to an end of your labour. I imagined that you had your hands pretty much full & never for a moment thought that I was forgotten, because you have not been able to write. It must have been a melancholy satisfaction to have been with poor Aunt Caroline at the last & she seems not to have suffered much pain & in her state one could not have wished her to remain…

I heard from Minnie this morning, she has a good deal of bother just now what with the children being laid up & not being able to get out, it makes them irritable. And then she is changing servants, which is always a lottery – I only hope she may find some soon to suit her. I regret this cough among them as of course the boys lose their schooling & Minnie is afraid that they will not be able to go till Easter, it will make them lose ground I doubt.

What a change in Mary Russell[1], how it must spoil her looks. I thought May would have been pretty but it is a very long time since I saw her. Russell himself I suppose is much as usual – has he done

---

[1] Mary Russell, 16 year old daughter of Champion Branfill Russell of Stubbers, North Ockendon. There was a close friendship between this family and the Fanshawes and after Mrs Catherine Fanshawe became a widow she became a regular guest at Stubbers – notably her presence was recorded there on the 1871 Census.

anything with the wildfowl[1] this winter - it ought to have been severe enough to please him?

I am very glad to find dearest Mother that you are able to do so much & feel none the worse for it – long may you continue so!

We are getting into the hot weather and I have the house shut up every morning at 9 o'clock & not opened till 5 – it keeps it cool & at night or rather towards morning, one is glad of a blanket – but I am afraid one cannot expect it very much longer. April & May are the worst months I hear. I continue all right, I am glad to say. I never touch anything till after racquets at night & have now come to a pint of claret at dinner & nothing after. I have one brandy & soda after racquets & that is all. My cold tea when I go to bed, *[this area smudged with blots]* excuse the blot I have no time to rewrite.

I am sorry to say Chadwick is going on 6 months leave to Cashmere[2] so I shall be all alone in my bungalow. To tell you the truth I am very tired of being separated from Minnie & children & for a very little would sell[3] tomorrow. All my old friends are away & I do not care for the country except for the rupees[4]. And Minnie seems so

---

[1] Champion Branfill Russell (1820 -1887) Lt Col. West Essex Militia, formerly Champion Branfill of Upminster Hall, took the name of Russell on inheriting the Stubbers estate about 5 miles east of Dagenham Village. He was an outstanding 'shot' and with a team of 32 gunners in 1860, secured the British record of 704 wild geese in one 'shoot'. Amongst many interests he is noted as a yachtsman, traveller and a pioneer of photography.

[2] Cashmere (Kashmir), the most northern region of South Asia. Prior to the Indian Rebellion of 1857, Cashmere implied only the valley between the Great Himalayas and the Pir Panjal mountain range but after Cashmere sided with the British, direct rule of this principality was assumed by Great Britain.

[3] The value of commissions varied by the regiment and levels of its social prestige. On retirement the sale of a commission provided an immediate source of capital/income.

[4] Rupee - monetary unit of India, from Sanskrit 'rūpya' - wrought silver, a coin of silver.

Kamptee, India (1894)
Worcestershire Regiment

Parade Ground at Kamptee, India
Worcestershire Regiment

unhappy that I hardly think it right to leave her alone & with all the children on her hands. I see the Royal Commissioners labours are not to be made known for another 2 or 3 months – I should like to know what they intend doing for us if anything, time will show! If I take full pay which I can apply for after 14ᵗʰ April I shall lose the money of my commissions for the children & I am not quite sure that selling altogether is not the best. I have no prospect of getting anything after my five years is up, beyond a depot centre & that would not suit my views in the least. I have been explicit with you but you need not tell anyone. I am saving money or would be home tomorrow!

I heard from Col. Beville[1] at Bombay, he has come out to this country again last month and is in Sinde[2]. He told me he had called on you before leaving. Many thanks for asking Robert Carey anything I want to know, he always is kind & willing to do anything he can. Pray remember me to him & thank him for his kind offer.

I suppose Lady Gosforth's[3] death will make a difference to Tiny[4] & she has small prospect of being a Peeress if Lord Gosforth marries…

I had a heavy time of it for about 3 weeks in writing for our inspection. I had to make 4 copies for every officer in the Regt. – so you may fancy I was pretty busy.

The General took five mornings at us & was pleased to be very complimentary – said he was agreeably surprised at the state he

---

[1] Colonel Henry Beville CB – Bombay Infantry.
[2] Sinde, a small principality in the Punjab.
[3] TBF made an error in the name – Lady Theodosia, widow of 3ʳᵈ Earl of <u>Gosford</u> died 13 February 1876 - her elder son, the 4ᵗʰ Earl of Gosford (1841-1922) married the following year.
[4] TBF's cousin, Clementina Mary Meysey Le Marchant, daughter of General Sir John Gaspard Le Marchant married in 1869, Maj-Gen. Hon. Edward Archibald Brabazon Acheson (1844-1921) younger brother of 4ᵗʰ Earl of Gosford.

found the Regt – far beyond his expectations judging from what he saw of it on its arrival & that I must have worked hard to get it so, which was satisfactory. What with the hot weather and the rains we shall not do much now till October.

I am sorry to say my Adjutant Conor[1] lost is wife last Tuesday, she was only ill a week, sore throat which became very bad & prevented her taking anything & getting sleep for fear of suffocation - & she sank I fancy from pure exhaustion. She leaves a baby out here about 6 or 8 months old & another child at home – I pity Conor very much, he is going home for a month's leave.

Mr Carpenter,[2] the head swell in the Civil Service, died last Monday at Nagpore, he was riding a steeple chase here this day fortnight, his horse fell with him at a fence & he [*inserted above*] Mr C was picked up insensible, never recovered & lingered till last Monday. He was a very able man & very popular – I did not know him, as he had only just come here.

I went into Nagpore on Tuesday & called on the Fanshawes. She is a bright cheerful person & I felt quite ashamed of having been here so long without going over. Now I know them, though I had met before, I suppose I shall see more of them. I like him & he is a great favourite at Nagpore.

---

[1] Lt Cecil Conor, 33rd Regiment served in the Abyssinia Expedition. Conor attended TBF's funeral so we must assume they stayed in contact after retirement.
[2] Charles Wilson Carpenter died on 5 March 1876 at the age of 39. A noted sportsman he had played first class cricket for his home county of Sussex.

I think Joe[1] is very wise in looking out for something to do & not leading an idle life. I wish Ned could find something & Evy. I hope his lady friend Lady Seabright[2] will perform her promise & find him some employment anywhere. I so hope Charlie will get a good station when his Reg't comes out here & that he will not dislike the country – I wish there was a little more shooting at this place. Chadwick & two others have been out the last week, but did not get very much – whether their fault or not I do not know. If I am here the next cold weather, I mean to try if I cannot do something in the shooting line.

I am glad you have heard from Dick again. I am so sorry he has to move just as he got his garden into shape. Hope his box will arrive all right & that your next accounts will give a better report of himself.

My horse the Arab you heard I had bought, is up to this a great success & one or two ladies in the Reg't particularly appreciate him as they are always asking me to lend him to ride. One lady said she was quite sorry she had ridden him as she was quite spoilt for any other horse in the place! He is a capital charger & very good looking & I only gave £80 for him.

Let me thank you very much for your kind wish about the money that comes to you from Aunt Caroline[3], whatever you like to do with it in any way, pray please yourself. I consider the money is yours. I shall be only too happy to let John have it. If you still insist

---

[1] Joseph Denison (1846-1917), Helen Denison's eldest son.
[2] Probably Olivia Amy Douglas Fitzpatrick, 3rd wife of Sir John Gage Saunders Seabright – married 1865 and lived at Eaton Place, Belgravia, London (died 1895).
[3] Letters of Administration granted 22 February 1876 by Principal Probate Registry to Mrs Catherine Fanshawe, sister and only next of kin of Caroline Somerville – effects listed as under £7,000.

on giving it me – whatever arrangements you may think fit to make I shall be perfectly content, as you have the sole control over it.

John wrote to me last week on the subject & I then told him if I could meet his wishes, I would gladly do so & still say so. So you may make his & your minds easy on the subject that whatever you decide upon doing will be right. I have made myself plain – now goodbye dearest Mother, with much love to all at Halkin Street & Wilton Place & same to self.

Ever your most affectionate son

Basil

I shall be glad to hear you have done what John wants –

Letter from Thomas Basil Fanshawe to his mother
Kamptee
Friday April 28th (1876)

My Dearest Mother,

Although the mail does not leave this till tomorrow I will begin today by thanking you for your last which reached me this morning – dated April 7th.

I am always pleased to hear from you & find out how things are going on. Yours & Minnie's were the only two that I received today & am glad to find the children are all on the mend & Bertie[1], who has been the worst has been able to get out & is picking up his appetite – but I suppose Minn keeps you au fait so I will not elicit a ~~double~~ [inserted] second citation.

We have so far got through our hot weather very fairly. It is hot of course, thermometer in mess house, where every appliance is in use to cool the place, stands about 90°. I see the maximum of the sun's rays at Allahabad[2], the shade of course, was 166°. I shall be very glad when we are at the end of next month or rather 10th June, by which time the rains ought to have begun.

Everyone has gone away from this that could get leave or had the money to do so. I have not found it as hot as Deesa yet, but of course do not know what next month may be like.

---

[1] Herbert Cecil Fanshawe – 2nd son of TBF was born 9th November 1867 in India - he served in Royal Engineer Militia (died 1952).

[2] Allahabad in Uttar Pradesh - original name – Prayag, 'the place of offerings' from its position at the confluence of the Ganga, Yamuna and Sarasvati rivers. It is the second-oldest city in India, and important in Hindu scriptures.

There is very little doing in the station just now, only one Badminton[1] night in the week at the Artillery mess – but I do not care for this & stick to my racquets – but do not begin until 4.30 instead of 3.30. It is warm work & one's racquet feels as if one had picked it up from an oven but I am quite sure it does one good. Our numbers are getting very small as some say it is too hot to walk over & play and I do not know what they do with themselves.

I am sorry to find the Bab thinks the infection of the whooping cough[2] may be given by our chicks to their house. No doubt she is on the safe side but I should have thought all danger would have been over.

It is very good & kind of you proposing the children should come up & be troubled with them, but perhaps they would, as you say, enjoy it more later on when able to get about more in longer days & let us hope, finer weather. I wish you had been able to say Minnie had promised to come up when they came. Mr Gosselin expected her to take the children away to the sea at Easter, the change would have no doubt done them all good, but I do not expect she will.

I hope you have been able to pay your visit to the Russells & did not forget to remember me. Any chance of her young ladies changing their names? Russell, I suppose just the same as ever? I heard Selina Gostling[3] was thinking of bringing Maria out to India by long sea for the benefit of her health but I should hardly think it would be put in

---

[1] Evolved from an older game called Battledore & Shuttlecock, Badminton was first played by the British in India from about 1870.

[2] Pertussis – usually called Whooping Cough because of the sound generated by exhausting coughing bouts. The highly infectious airborne bacterium Bordetella Pertussis spreads easily within the first 3 weeks of illness. Treatment with antibiotics and a vaccination programme of prevention after the middle of twentieth century have substantially reduced the numbers of cases.

[3] Selina A M C Gostling (née Stonhouse) aged 41, widow of a 1st cousin of TBF, Charles Philips Gostling a civil servant who served in the Civil Service in Madras.

practice – am sorry to hear Maria[1] is so delicate. How does Harry[2] get on in the Royals?

I have seen nothing more of the Arthur Fanshawe's at Nagpore, he is busy all day in office and the correct calling hour in this country is the hottest part of the day, between 12 & 2 & a nine miles drive before & after the visit. I wanted him to come over & stop a night or two with me & he said he would but as yet has not carried out his promise.

My friend Chadwick started on the 8th of this month for Cashmere & I heard from him a few days ago, saying his luggage that he had sent on previous to leaving this – had not turned up & his warm clothing, fishing tackle etc., were not forthcoming. He could not replace them for love or money – could not wait for their arrival, as if they did not push on at once, they could in all probability find their intended route disturbed. It must have been very provoking as he was looking forward to the fishing for Mahaseer in the Jehlum River[3].

I find it very lonely in the bungalow – parade at six, office work till about 8 when I get back to my house, make my toilet for the day, then to mess about 10, where I remain till 12 o/c – on return here read till it is time to go to racquets & dinner at eight.

Chadwick will not be back till October, he finds that as far as he has gone his expenses are greater than he expected. One of my fellows is

---

[1] Mrs Agnes Maria Lethbridge wife of Henry St. John Vaughan Le Marchant married 1866.

[2] Henry St. John Vaughan Le Marchant – Royal Artillery, Lt. Colonel on retirement in 1885 – son of Sir John Gaspard Le Marchant & 1st cousin to TBF.

[3] River Jehlam, a tributary of the Chenab River is 725 kilometres long and flows through both India and Pakistan. It is the most westerly of the five rivers of the Punjab.

out after tiger but done nothing, though he killed a bear[1] & two more are going through, though I fancy they have not much chance of tigers unless they go with some big civilian & they will have to go some 150 miles before they have a chance. This weather in tents would prove rather trying, do you not think so? We have been having wonderful cool nights & mornings. I sleep under a punkah[2] & manage to sleep all right, I am glad to say.

Saturday

Last Night the thermometer at mess was 95° and it is pretty warm today.

I have heard nothing more from Edward Le Marchant in 67th though I wrote to him some time ago. He told me he was going on detachment to Trichinoploy[3], rather a hot place I believe – not much chance of our meeting.

I hope you have heard again from Dick & of the safe arrival of the box. Minnie told me that young Elkington[4] had called on you & told you what he could about Dick.

So Joe is off to the California – rather unexpected was it not? But I am quite sure that he is right. I shall be glad to hear Ned & Evy had both got something to do, whatever it was – a hard matter in these times!

---

[1] Himalayan Black Bear or India Black Bear.
[2] Large cloth fan on a frame suspended from a ceiling and worked by a cord.
[3] Trichinopoly, a district of the Madras Presidency of British India and the princely state of Pudukkottai remained within the jurisdiction of the district from 1865 to 1947. The area is one of the oldest inhabited regions of South India with archaeological evidence of Stone Age dwelling.
[4] Probably Arthur Guy Elkington, Surgeon Major (South Fusilier Guards) whose address at Bath was close to TBF's home.

Will you kindly tell Helen that I have been making enquiries about the gold braid for embroidery she wished for & am informed that English made braid is far away superior to anything to be got in this country. She must not fancy that I am unwilling to get it. I shall only try to get anything she wishes but I must have a pattern to guide me – Chadwick would get it for me easily.

I am afraid this is about as stupid a production as it well could be but you must take the will for the deed, we have nothing stirring to tell you about.

My best love to all in Halkin Street & Wilton Place & with the same to yourself ever dearest Mother.

Your most affectionate son

Basil

An additional note from Thomas Basil Fanshawe to his mother, enclosed with the previous letter:

<u>Private</u>

I have not alluded in my letter to anything about the money, as you can show it if you like & burn this. I am very pleased at what you tell me, dearest Mother that I shall not be called upon to pay either interest or capital. I am quite happy to do this both if required. Truly I should like to know & not have such a claim as over £400 nearer £500 made against me at any future time. It is not that I think or rather thought the claim unfair or unjust ~~but~~ as I agreed to pay the interest, but I did think that I ought to have been told that I was liable for the interest & should have to pay it. I could have taken steps to pay it or reduce it by degrees.

However thanks to your great kindness about Aunt Caroline's money, that appears not to be necessary. I cannot tell you how much obliged I am for your devoting the money to that purpose. I am afraid you have been robbing yourself. I do hope you will let me know if you want anything for Dick. I shall be only too glad to assist.

I decided nothing yet about my future, am waiting to hear from Bath. I should like if possible to remain out till July next or August, then get 15 months leave & come home, which would complete my time for full Colonel & I would be eligible for anything going – or if I thought better, retire. The only drawback is the hot weather.

Of course I have said nothing about this to Minnie so please do not – nor have I said anything about the money or interest, so I should not if I was you – but you can please yourself.

John Gaspard Fanshawe (1824 – 1903)
LBBD Archives at Valence House

Mrs Caroline Somerville née Le Marchant (1802 – 1876)
Photograph of an original sketch
LBBD Archives at Valence House

I can only say how much obliged I am to you for this freeing me of the claim. I shall always be glad to help John in anyway & glad to hear that things are mending with him & that no more repairs will be required.

With best love ever dearest Mother, your affectionate son

Basil

Letter from Thomas Basil Fanshawe to his mother
Kamptee
Friday May 26th (1876)

My Dearest Mother,

The mail of May 4th from England brought me yours of that date this morning. Many thanks for your long letter & for Dick's which I now return. Am glad to find he is so pleased with all the articles the box contained – what a heavy charge to make for the box, to absorb nearly £5 and the things seem to have been just what he wished for and wanted most.

I should be very pleased to hear he accepted the offer made him by the Russells of going to the Cape[1] to look after their newly bought property. It sounds swell & I hope it may turn out so, it would set Dick on his legs again & be, I should imagine just that sort of thing he could like. I hope his foot will soon get all right again.

John's letter which he told you he had written to me, & I thought odd not having got, turned up last mail not having put anything on it (via so & so), it came by Southampton. Only took 6 weeks instead of 19 days! He gives good accounts of all his belongings.

Am glad you had a good time of it as the Yankees say, with the Russells – a regular family gathering. Is that Major Boycott[2] who Edith[3] is going to marry, a man who was in the 17th Reg't, I fancy I know the name although I cannot quite recollect him?

---

[1] Cape Town, South Africa.

[2] Major William Boycott 29th Regiment – died in Africa approximately 1885.

[3] Mary Edith Way (1848 – 1927) a daughter of Revd C J Way, Spaynes Hall, Yeldham, and late Vicar of Yeldham. Mrs Emily Augusta Russell (née Way) wife of Champion Russell was her cousin.

Rather a sudden fancy for the Russells to take a trip to the Cape? I only hope the property he goes to see will come up to his expectation & form a success for both him & Dick. I dare say, Mrs Russell will be charmed with the trip – how long do they go for?

Now for a little about myself, we are so far well thro' the hot weather & another fortnight we ought to be much in the rains. We had a most delicious thunder storm last Wednesday, about 4 o'clock in the afternoon & though it did not last long, half an hour, it had a wonderful effect in cooling the air & ground. We had about half an inch of rain in the time. The trees look quite fresh after it. I thought we should have had another last night – the wind got up & it looked very like another but to our disgust it blew off, except a few drops. There has been no rain since October last, except one shower on 13th March, so you may imagine how the ground sucked it up. There was hardly a sign of it on the roads at home afterwards. People say it is the working up of the Monsoon[1] which they prophecy is to be very early this year. I am sure I hope so, one gets very tired of the heat at somewhere between 90° & 100° indoors for two months. What it is outside, I leave your to imagine - 122° the highest though. I think Deesa was hotter than this. I am sure & everyone agrees with me in thinking so – that was hell!

I have stuck steadily to racquets every day & am quite sure that I have felt the heat less than those who take no exercise. I still stick to my same amount of liquid, 1 brandy & soda after playing & half a bottle of claret at dinner. I ride of a morning on parade & when I am Field Officer[2] – which comes around pretty often as there are so few of us present here, everyone gone away on leave.

---

[1] The word first used in English in British India – referring to the big seasonal winds blowing from the Bay of Bengal and the Arabian Sea in the southwest, bringing heavy rainfall to the area.

[2] A military officer holding the 'field' rank of major, lieutenant-colonel, or colonel.

You ask me whether I am saving. I am glad to say that I am - about £100 a month, which is something, but you need not mention the same. ~~It~~ Is it not too hard, it costs me by the rate of exchange nearly £15 in every £100 to send it home? That is for every £100 I send from here, I only get 85 at home. It is ruinous & not only harshest of the exchange getting home for us, the Gov't allow the soldiers to remit at 2/- & a ½ for the rupees, but not officers.

That Pyretic Saline[1] is first rate stuff if one is not quite right, I have half a bottle left of it. Should you have a chance, I should be very glad of another. I am glad to say, I have not been obliged to have recourse to it often. My liver has not troubled me much I am glad to say & I have had nothing to complain of so far.

I have a companion now in the house with me, our last joined Lieut. who came to us from the Militia - a nice boy of the name of Garnett[2]. I believe they come from Lancashire, close to where our property[3] was but they do not live there now. Roman Catholic & well off, I imagine. The house is not nearly so dull.

I have heard from Chadwick who had reached Kashmir - the correct way of spelling it nowadays - & who was charmed with the climate & scenery. The only drawback, the prevalence of cholera[4] which he trusted he might escape & so do I. I expect he goes home for good

---

[1] Effervescent Pyretic Saline, a patent medicine made by Henry Lamplough of Holborn, London. Advertised as a remedy for cholera, smallpox, skin conditions, sea sickness and headaches, as well as preventing tropical and colonial diseases.

[2] Lt. Henry Percy Garnett, 33rd Regiment – of Moor Hall, Sutton Coldfield.

[3] Swainshead in Wyersdale Lancashire.

[4] During the nineteenth century, cholera spread across the world from its original reservoir in the Ganges delta in India. Six subsequent pandemics have killed millions of people across all continents. An extremely virulent disease affecting children and adults, it takes from 12 hours to 5 days to show symptoms after contaminated food or water has been ingested and if treatment is not given death can occur within hours. Today, good sanitation, hygiene and modern oral cholera vaccines help control this disease.

next year & I hope I may manage to get home at the same time. I told you in my last what my ideas were on the subject of leaving the army…

I wonder where the 100[th][1] will go to on arrival in this country? Nowhere near us, I expect - how does Charlie like the idea of coming out? I hope Ned will have more success than has hitherto attended his efforts with the machine for raising ships[2]. How hard it seems to get employment. Evy still without job seems to have had a pleasant trip[3] to the other side of the world – how long does he think of stopping over there? He will do well, more than I imagine Seymour [Le Marchant] in Guernsey will do from all accounts - they are a queer family! I am sorry you give such a bad report of Maria what a source of anxiety she must be to her mother. How does Harry[4] get on in the Royals – well I hope?

I should rather like to see a prospectus of the college[5] near Oxford for sons of officers that you mention, it sounds well. There is a similar institution at Westward Ho[6] to which I was very nearly belonging – but the latter was for boys up to a certain age & the one you mention I should think was more for young men.

---

[1] 100th (Yeomanry) Regiment Royal Artillery.

[2] Edward Fanshawe Denison was to become a founding partner of Simpson Denison & Co, Marine Engineers of Dartmouth, Devon.

[3] Evelyn Fanshawe applied for a passport in 1876 but his destination of travel is not known.

[4] Henry St. John Vaughan Le Marchant 14th Brigade Royal Artillery retired 1885 with rank of Lt Colonel – 1st cousin to TBF.

[5] Oxford Military College opened in September 1876.

[6] United Services College opened in 1874 - a boys' public boarding school for the sons of military officers preparing for military service. The college merged with Imperial Service College in 1906, and in 1942 merged further with Haileybury College, Herts (alumni includes Rudyard Kipling).

I will not mention any home news as Minnie no doubt keeps you well up in their doings. It is very kind of you thinking of having the 3 eldest up to form acquaintance with their cousins. I hope they will give you no trouble, if they do pay you a visit.

I am afraid I shall get no fishing this year (the Mahaseer), as my friend who asked me was unable to go, as his wife has just been confined - but I hope I may catch a fish someday.

I should not have thought it a very wise proceeding on Ө Gostlings part, buying land & building a house but I presumed everyone knows their own affairs but pray remember me to Robert Carey. Any hints on the Royal Commission so long delayed, as to what way we are likely to be touched by it - that he can pick up, I shall be glad to hear & he is a man on the spot who would hear most things said on this topic?

I have not the slightest chance of a brigade for another 10 or 15 years, they only fall to the lot of full Colonels & of considerable standing & as I shall not, if I live till 1878, be a full Colonel till then. I am sure John will agree with me that a chance of a brigade command falling to my lot is remote in the extreme, at any rate for many years - and I think the older one gets, the less one is suited for this climate!

I heard the other day from Edward Le Marchant in 67th, he is now at Madras, part of the regiment there & part gone up with the Colonel to Bhamo[1] as escort to the commissioner about Margary[2] murder.

---

[1] Bhamo, a city of Kachin State in the northernmost part of Myanmar (Burma), located 116 miles south from the capital city of the state of Kachin on the Ayeyarwady River, within 40 miles of the border with Yunnan Province, China.

[2] Margary murder or 'Affair' - a crisis in Sino-British relations which followed the murder in 1875 of British diplomat Augustus Raymond Margary whilst exploring new trade routes from Shanghai through southwest China to Bhamo in Upper Burma.

E.L regrets much that he was not with that part of the Reg't, he would have seen a new country at any rate.

I see Gaspard Tupper[1] is coming out to India at the end of the year. I wonder where he will fall? I thought he would come if he had a chance – does Mary[2] come with him?

St John Thomas[3] seems to be in a queer state – if he leaves his wife[4] at home to spend his money, he might as well remain in England. His brother seems to have fallen on hard lines in having to sell his place & losing his wife, but perhaps the latter may be a gain!

You must be quite tired with hearing all this rubbish so in mercy to you will stop.

With best love to all in Halkin Street & Wilton Place and the same to yourself, ever dearest mother

Your most affectionate son

Basil

Did Minnie tell you that Mrs Dunlop, her old nurse had lost her husband[5] from heat apoplexy out here a short time ago? I lost two more sergeants from the same cause this week. I pity the widows & children so much, gov't allows rations & a certain amount of money for 12 months & then if they do not marry, gives them a passage home.

---

[1] Colonel Gaspard Le Marchant Tupper, Royal Horse Artillery, on retirement Lt. General & Colonel Commandant of the Regiment & KB (1905) - son of Eliza Le Marchant and TBF's 1st cousin.

[2] Mrs Mary Charlotte Tupper (née Smith) married 1861.

[3] Colonel Henry St. John Thomas Le Marchant, Royal Artillery retired 1889 - TBF's 1st cousin.

[4] Agnes Maria Pursell married 1866.

[5] 20th April 1876 – Sergeant John Dunlop of 33rd Regiment died aged 44 at Kamptee.

(An additional note accompanying the previous letter)

Thomas Basil Fanshawe to his mother

<u>Strictly Private – Burn it when read</u>

Let me thank you very much dearest Mother for all your kind intentions towards me & Minnie with regard to Aunt Caroline's property that falls to your share – I am glad to think it will be also be a help to John. By the way I have not heard from John since his letter of February 11th which reached me on 3rd March – so he must have forgotten the date when he told you he had written the mail previous to your last of April 7th.

I want to tell you, between ourselves of what my plans are. I wrote to Mr Gosselin some 3 weeks ago on the subject & he ought to be getting the letter now. Minnie is so wretched & unhappy that I am half inclined to cut the whole thing & come home. It is no use my hanging on for anything in the army, I have not been lucky enough & it is now a question shall I sell or go on full pay & when. I should in all probability get about £5000 for selling which would be something for the children - & the other way I should get about £1800 down & £365 a year which of course would lapse at my death. I should I imagine be thus rather better off as regards income than by selling out but should have no money to leave.

If I could manage it, I should like if my health stands & I hope it may – remain out here till next July & than get 15 months leave to England & then decide at home.

You seem to think dearest Mother that I am an evergreen. I am getting on completed 30 years' service on the 14th on the month and I am getting rather tired of knocking about the world. I should not be a full Colonel till September 1878 – a long time yet.

I do not mean to remain another hot season out here anyhow, I have now had enough of it & should I get seedy[1], back I come at once.

The depot centres would never suit me, I am daily tempted to send in my papers to sell – all my old pals are gone. Of course I have settled nothing & request you will not hint a word to anyone. I dare not tell Minnie as it would be such a bitter disappointment if any delay arose.

Again thanking you for all you kind proposals about Aunt C property – why do you not make use of it yourself?

Yours affectionate son

Basil

---

[1] Unwell.

Letter from Thomas Basil Fanshawe to his mother
Kamptee
Tuesday June 27th (1876)

My Dearest Mother,

I will begin my letter to you today, though the mail does not leave till tomorrow. The steamer leaves Bombay with the English mails on a Friday now during the monsoon, instead of Monday & I suppose such an arrangement will hold good till after monsoon is over in Sept. Of course under these circumstances we never get our English letters in time to reply by the outgoing mail.

Yours of June 1st reached me last week on the 23rd. Many thanks for it. I am glad to say that all the intense heat is over & thereafter we have not had any very heavy bursts of rain. We have had some 5 inches or so which has done a deal of good. I am Field Officer today & got caught in a shower going round this morning the guards – which wetted me in my white clothing very quick. I changed as soon as I got home. The rain has rather interrupted with our racquets as it generally comes on in afternoon & spoils our fun as the court is an open one, but one must not complain it is much pleasanter weather than it was a month back & only a difference of some 35° in the temperature – having gone down from 115° & 120° to 80° & 85°.

People are beginning to come back & I am not sorry as there are very few Field Officers to do duty now but I suppose we shall get them back by degrees. The General returned about 10 days ago. I am going to dine with him tomorrow night & I dined out on Saturday at a Dr Theobald's[1] who is the head doctor of native troops here - a party of six only, his wife[2], the rest officers – & though the dinner was good it was very slow. I suppose people will think of giving

[1] Henry Theobald, Apothecary, Madras Medical Department, Kamptee.
[2] Catherine Jane Clifford married 18th June 1834 – Bangalore, Madras, India.

dinners again now the hot weather is over. It would have been simply purgatory.

I saw the thermometer mark 100° at the mess table one night, with every appliance for cooling the atmosphere that one could have at work. Of course we did not often have it so high but anything under 95° we considered cool <u>inside</u> the house. I had 15 men taken into hospital from the heat one afternoon & most of them I am glad to say recovered. The more I see of the country, the less I like it.

I heard from Chadwick not long ago. His things turned up all right at last but they were a long time about it, he does not return till October. My other major, Weeding is also away on leave.

It is very kind of you thinking of having the children up with you during their holidays, which I suppose are, or are about to commence. I hope Minnie will be persuaded to take them up to you, I am sure the change would do her good. She tells me all the Chicks have coughs but otherwise flourishing – I want her if she does not go up to you, to go for a little change to the seaside somewhere with the others instead of remaining in Bath all the summer & Bath is generally hot. She gives a good account of all at 28 except Lizzy but as you no doubt know more about them & later, I won't repeat.

Many thanks for saying you will get an acknowledgement from John for the money. I consider dearest Mother, the money is your own. You have complete power of disposal of it I imagine & I am very grateful for your kind wishes on my behalf. If Aunt Caroline had left me the money by will it would have been different & it caused you a lot of trouble, how glad you will be when everything connected with the settlement of her affairs is wound up.

I hope Dick will accede to the Russell's offer, you have not had time to hear again from him?

I see Evy was presented at a drill[1] lately. I suppose he thinks it a good thing over. I quite agree with Robert Carey that the Royal Commission will not do much good to any ranks among the officers, the juniors if any one benefits will reap most advantage. It is a great shame keeping one so long in suspense but I suppose Mr Hardy[2] was afraid to bring forward any measure on its accommodation this year & so shelved it till quite the end of the session, too late to legislate on it.

Aunt Julia[3] is a wonderful woman. I saw Sir G Hewett's[4] death in the paper, he leaves a large family but poorly provided for from your account.

I wish you had been able say uncle H Lefevre's[5] nose was mending – but he seems all right otherwise. I have heard of Robert Le Marchant[6] being ill. Edward his son in 67th at Madras & I exchange a letter now and again, it would be a very serious thing for his family if anything happened to him. Dan Tupper[7] seems to rub on much as usual.

---

[1] Evelyn John Fanshawe joined the West Essex Militia on 30th March 1875. Attaining the rank of Captain in 1881 he resigned his commission in 1887.

[2] Gathorne Gathorne-Hardy, 1st Earl of Cranbrook (1814 – 1906), Conservative politician who held cabinet office appointments between 1858 and 1892. He was Secretary of State for War (1874 - 1878) when he oversaw the army reforms initiated by Edward Cardwell, his Liberal predecessor.

[3] Louisa Julia Ann Hewett – born 1817, daughter of Col. Sir G H Hewett 2nd Bt. & Louise Majendie.

[4] Twice married and father of 10 children, Sir George J R Hewett 3rd Bt. – died 15th April 1876.

[5] Henry Shaw-Lefevre (1802 – 1880) was TBF's uncle by his marriage to Helen Le Marchant.

[6] Rev'd Robert Le Marchant died aged 95 - 12th February 1915.

[7] Daniel Tupper (died 1879), husband of Anna Maria La Marchant, parents of Gaspard, Æmilius & Eliza Tupper – TBF's uncle by marriage.

Helen told me that Mr Smith Dorrien[1] had been seriously ill & does not seem by your report to get much better. I hold he will soon gain strength. I hope Joe Denison will find California to his mind & get plenty of paying employment. I wonder how Charlie will like this country? Helen's cold has I trust departed & hope she will enjoy her trip to Scilly – she must be comforted at the idea of Katie getting all right eventually.

Among our trials now, are the swarms of insects, beetles [and] white ants which drop their wings on the table, & other pests which make their appearance at the dinner table – attracted by the light & then one either gets bitten or the change of weather brings out spots, which look like bites & they are very irritating & one cannot help rubbing them, which of course makes them worse.

I sent back on Sunday the horse Colonel Dance lent me, as his leave was up & he wants it. So it departed for Secunderabad[2], a four days journey (night & day) from here - so now I have only my Arab. I still stick to racquets & have done so all the hot weather & am sure the exercise has kept me well.

I wish my letters were as long & as worth reading as yours are but there is little or nothing to write about from this, one day is so like another & you frequently have fellows say thank God another day is gone when they come to mess, which does not look as if they cared for the country much does it?

Now goodbye, with best love to you & all at Wilton Place & Halkin Street.

---

[1] Robert Algernon Smith Dorrien of Haresfoot, Berkhampstead, Herts. Captain 3rd Light Dragoons and 16th Lancers &, Colonel Herts Militia (1814 – 1879) & Mary Ann Smith Dorrien, his wife (1825 – 1909).
[2] Secunderabad-Wadi Line completed and opened October 1874 being the first railway in Hyderabad.

Ever dearest Mother,

Your affectionate son

Basil

The mail arrived in Bombay yesterday, so we ought to get our letters tomorrow…

Letter from Thomas Basil Fanshawe to his mother
Kamptee
July 19th (1976)

My Dearest Mother,

Many thanks for your last long letter of June 23rd which reach me last week just after our mail for England had been despatched. I am glad to find you had so many visitors to amuse you. Your adventures with the cab men bringing you home after dining out could not have been pleasant. I should hire a brougham[1] in future. I wish you would, & let me pay for them. I should only be too pleased to think I had saved you any discomfort or annoyance.

Many thanks, dearest Mother for so kindly thinking of me and ordering a fresh supply of pyretic saline & lemon kali[2]. It has not yet reached me for I suppose it will come via Southampton & your letter came via Brindisi[3]. The saline is first rate stuff if one is a little out of order which one can easily be in this country at the best of times, though thank goodness I continue all right & trust I may do so, as long as I remain out.

I have still some of the saline left though it is getting low & a bottle of Kali. I still go on with racquets & drinking the same amount daily as I did in the hot weather – also thanks for the prospectus of the Oxford college.

---

[1] Brougham - lightweight, four-wheeled horse-drawn carriage first built for Lord Brougham around 1840. Able to turn sharply, the coach was suited to cities and had two seats facing forward with a window to see ahead whilst the driver & footman sat on a box seat at the front.

[2] Lemon kali – artificially flavoured carbonated lemon drink or Sherbet Lemon.

[3] Brindisi - chosen by the P & O Steam Navigation Co. for their European terminus port to India via the Suez Canal. From 1871 to 1914 the Indian Mail Route stopped at Brindisi. Passengers & cargo travelled out from London to Brindisi by rail and transferred onto ships sailing every Sunday at 2 p.m. to Port Said, Bombay and Calcutta.

With regard to Robert Carey's advice it is very good but what prospect have I of ever getting anything beyond a Brigade depot? I am in my 31ˢᵗ years' service and nearly 47. I am afraid the Essex Constabulary[1] would never do, I am not eligible, too old! I think the first thing done by the magistrates in making their selection, is to eject all candidates over 40 or 42, so I am out of that! Though especially obliged by your making it & thinking it would suit.

After the knocking about I have had so many years, I begin to think I might rest quiet & remain out here separated from Minnie & the children. I won't do much longer – I am getting quite miserable & longing to be home. Of course all I say is intended for you alone. At any rate at present, if I find I can manage to rub on at home on what I have, I do not see the good of remaining. I must sell out some day or other to assure the money for my children - & it is only a question of retiring on full pay or selling. I have written to know what I should get in either case & then shall consult Minnie & Mr Gosselin as to which they think would be most advisable. Of course I shall see if this Royal Commission will do anything for us but agree with R Carey in thinking that nothing good will come for men in my position.

This is not a fit country for a Christian! I heard yesterday of the death of my junior Major Weeding[2] from Cholera at Ahmedabad in the Bombay Presidency, poor fellow – only ill two days, he was away on two month's leave – very sad is it not? The Reg't has lost a

---

[1] The Essex Police Constabulary was formed in 1840.

[2] Weeding, Alexander James, Major - 33ʳᵈ Regiment. Cause of death recorded as Cholera on 14ᵗʰ July 1876 at Ahmedabad, he was buried the following day. Probate granted to his widow Elizabeth Weeding.

number of sergeants & men at the end of the hot weather, from heat apoplexy[1].

Thank goodness we are now well into the rains & it is pouring as I am writing & has been off & on since Saturday last, the 15th. You have no idea of how refreshing it is & how green & fresh everything looks & the new vegetation that springs up. One can hardly believe it is the same place it was a month back with the ground as yellow as a deal board & about as hard. A light blanket over one at night is really comfortable but I still have a punkah going to keep off mosquitoes & insects. There is one small species of fly, hardly visible which worries one & bites as much as a mosquito & you do not feel the brute till after he has bit or stung you. One has just paid a visit on the back of my left hand, resulting in its destruction I am glad to say – but leaving two big marks as a memento, to which I have just applied ammonia[2], the best thing out to relieve the pain & irritation.

I have not seen Mrs Dunlop[3] since her husband's death. I am rather surprised she has not paid me a visit. She is still matron in the female hospital & has been far from well but is now all right again.

I have six widows & their children on the strength of the Reg't, their husband's having died since we came out. Poor things, they receive a certain amount for themselves & children monthly & if they do not marry again before 12 months have expired, Gov't provide them with a passage home.

---

[1] Heatstroke was highly dangerous in excessively hot climates where the military had long exposed duties and marched great distances. If the body's heat balance becomes impaired, severe heatstroke abruptly sets in and leads to a loss of consciousness, convulsions, rapid and shallow breathing. The blood circulation slows and elevation of the body temperature to 41°– 42°C could be fatal even when young, fit and healthy, unless treated urgently.
[2] Ammonia (NH_3), colourless, pungent gas composed of nitrogen and hydrogen.
[3] Mary Ann Dunlop (born 1828), widow of Sgt. John Dunlop 33rd Regiment.

The rupee has gone down lately, at a most rapid & ruinous rate. One loses a fourth of what one sends home, that is the rupee is only worth 1/6d instead of two shillings – so if you want to send £100 home, only £75 is paid to whom you send it. People are crying out & justly so about this grievance & declare Gov't ought to interfere in the matter & either allow officers to remit to their families at 2/- the rupee or increase their pay to make it equal. Neither of which, I suppose it will do.

I get 4½ per cent for money on deposit here, I live in hopes of the rupee getting up again before I leave the country, if I ever do…

I hope Dick will agree to the Cape proposal, it sounds well & just the thing he would like, I imagine. What a time it takes to get an answer from him, I should think his leg would not stand in his way, for he could always ride & horses are or were cheap at the Cape. I am now with only one - my Arab, having sent back the other to his owner, Colonel Dance at Secunderabad[1] in the Deecan and have heard of it's safe arrival & the owner's joy at receiving it in such good condition. He sent me a most complimentary letter. One horse is quite enough for the work I have & should not have bought two, but having this one lent before I owned one, I could not back out of it, nor could I throw away the chance of purchasing the Arab. I should never have got so good an opportunity.

Chadwick writes to me pretty regularly, telling me his thoughts, he has had little sport with either game or rod & his butler (servant) - head servants in Bombay are so called, has turned out a robber & a drunkard, so he has turned him off. Most inconvenient, where he is as he cannot replace him. Chadwick found he charged 75 per cent

---

[1] Secunderabad – Located in the State of Telangana, and the twin city of Hyderabad. Founded as a British Cantonment in 1806 a British culture developed making the area distinctly different to Hyderabad.

on all articles of food he got & as the man got an anna in the rupee (16 annas in the rupee) from the tradespeople besides on any rupee expended, he must have done a good stroke of business while it lasted. As I dine at mess, my butler has not the same chance, should he be so disposed, but so far I have been lucky in my domestics.

Young Garnett who lives in the bungalow with me wants two months leave to go to Simla[1] to see his brother[2] who commands the 11th Hussars, so I shall be alone again till October when both he & Chadwick will return almost together. Whether we three shall continue to live together remains to be seen. Garnett will have to go if anyone.

Poor Weeding's death will give Johnstone[3] promotion as they cannot pass him over & this will take him from the depot at Chatham, out here. I suppose the step will compensate for leaving home, I am afraid the senior Lieutenant will not get a step, as we have two Captains to be absorbed.

Thank John for his message when you meet, glad to hear Harry is doing so well with his Reg't. Poor Maria seems to suffer more frequently from those attacks. Malta is their destination for the winter, I hear.

---

[1] After 1876 Simla (or Shimla) became the HQ of Indian Army and Government during the hot season. The town had an ideal climate and living soon became very expensive due to limited accommodation. Wives and daughters of British men stayed in Shimla whilst husbands remained on the plains. 'Shimla Society' was made up of these lone women and many unattached bachelor merchants and soldiers causing the resort to gain a reputation for gossip and stories of infidelity.
[2] Albert Peel Garnet Lt. Col, - 11th Hussars (b1837), migrated to Tasmania in 1882 and died in Windsor, Berks 1906.
[3] Captain John Douglas Johnstone (1836 – 1906) 33rd Regiment who later retired with the rank of Colonel, Royal Sussex Regiment - was the son of Major General John D. Johnstone of the 33rd Regiment.

I hope you will be able to join Minnie at the seaside where I hope she intends to take the children & give them a complete change it will do them all good & I think take away all the remains of the coughs, which still hangs about Bertie & baby. As you no doubt, correspond pretty frequently I would enter not into their doing…

Neither Helen nor John have favoured me lately, tell the former that Chadwick will try to get her gold thread at Agra[1] or Delhi on the way back, but she must wait for it.

With much love to all at both houses & the same to yourself,

Ever dearest Mother,

Your most affectionate son

Basil

Mind - I look on the brougham arrangement as settled, let me know the amount when the bill comes in…

Has Evy got anything to do yet, or Ned?

---

[1] Agra lies on the banks of the River Yamuna, in the northern state of Uttar Pradash and is 128 miles south of Delhi –the Taj Mahal is located in this city.

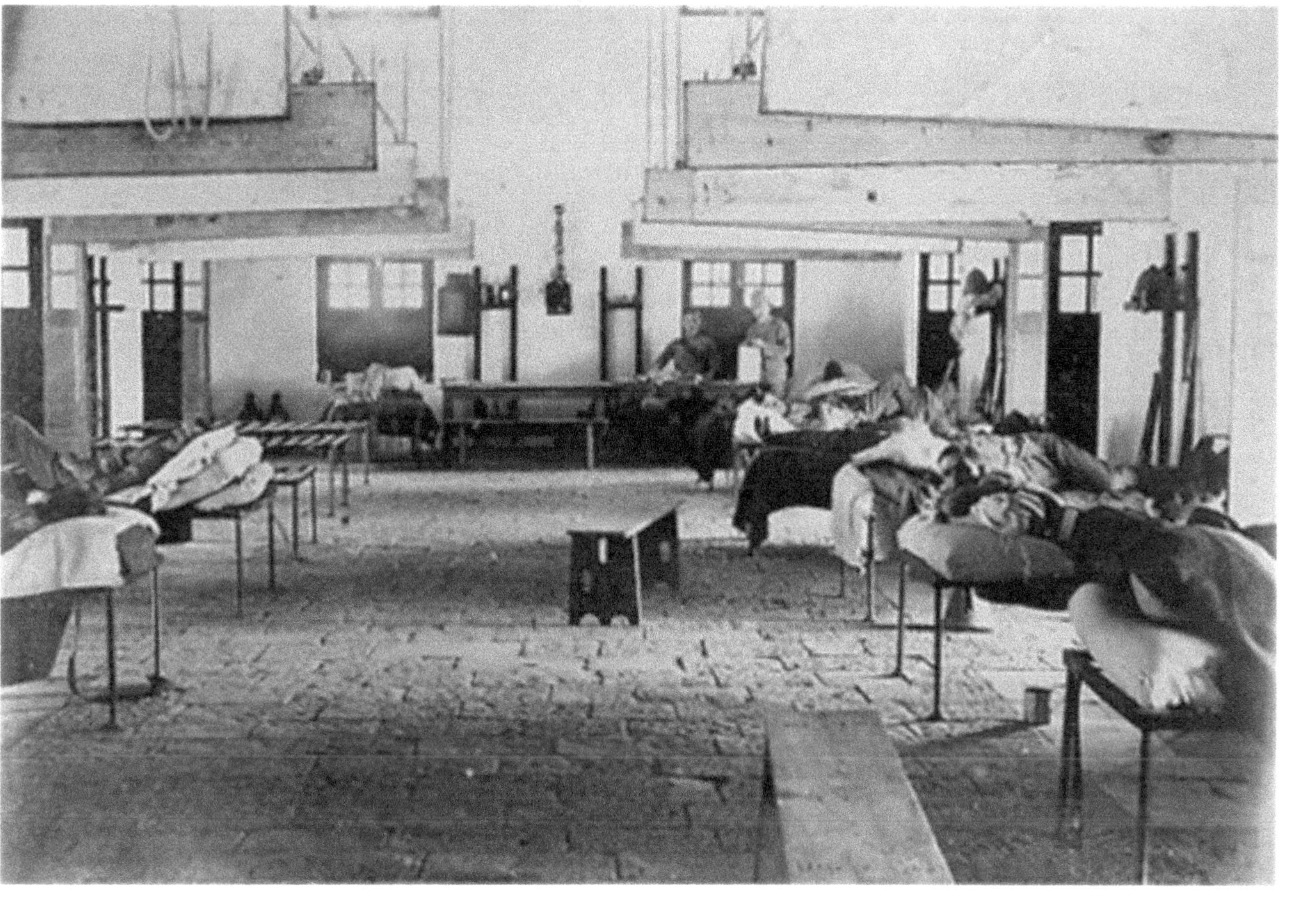

Guard Room, Kamptee, India
Worcestershire Regiment

Recreation Room and Theatre - English mail just arrived
Worcestershire Regiment

Letter from Thomas Basil Fanshawe to his mother
Kamptee
August 15th (1876)

My Dearest Mother,

Although our mail does not leave till tomorrow for Bombay to take the English boat on Friday, I will begin my letter today.

First let me thank you for your last of July 20th which reached me last Thursday and for the pyretic saline & lemon kali which reached me earlier in the week from Bradley & Bourdas[1], two bottles of saline & one of Kali, a most abundant supply & so well packed that nothing was cracked even. I have still a supply of the former bottle left so I shall now be well off – many thanks for sending it to me.

I have a hat from Lock[2] in St. James Street on its way out & only hope it will arrive as safely as the bottles did. I cannot get a hat here, if I could I should put up with it, but I cannot.

I was glad to find by yours that you enjoyed the change at New Lodge[3], after London heat & dust which (the heat) seems to have been nearly tropical & the appliances to relieve it small. I imagine your delight in being in a garden again among the flowers.

You are quite right in saying that the heat was much like what we have if the thermometer reached so many degrees, but I expect it was only in the day time & it went down again at night & you had cool nights. Not like what we have, it is seldom under 90° indoors

---

[1] Bradley & Bourdas, Chemists - 6 Pont Street, Belgrave Square, London SW1.

[2] Lock & Co, Hatters of St. James Street. London opened in 1764 - makers of Wellington's hat worn at the Battle of Waterloo in 1815 and the commissioners of the first bowler hat from Thomas Bowler in 1849.

[3] The Hertfordshire home of Frances Isabella Le Marchant (née Smith), widow of Colonel Thomas Le Marchant, (1811 – 1873) - younger brother of Mrs Catherine Fanshawe.

for 2½ months – it begins to get monotonous. I saw the mercury up at 100° at the mess table one night & from 95° to 98° our average temperature in the mess room. We have nothing to complain of in our weather it is pleasant enough for this vile country. I am sick of it, one is able to get about and have all ones doors & windows open. More rain is wanted for the crops, otherwise there will be a failure which means increased prices & with the rupee down to 1/8d in sending home money it will be no joke.

I have been much as usual, I am thankful to say & trust I may continue so. I am very prudent & make no difference now in exercise & food to what I did in the hot weather.

I hope you will be able to arrange to join Minnie & chicks at the seaside at Budleigh Salterton[1] – a little change to the sea would do you no harm. I expect Minnie chose that place as it was easier to get at than the north of Devon and with so many to move & only herself to do it, it was a consideration. In one of her letters she talked of Mr G Gosselin having an idea of going also. I hope he may, possibly Mr & Mrs Gosselin may go later but Mrs Gosselin does not like moving – but I am forgetting that you will know a good deal more about their movements than I can tell you.

It is very good of you dearest Mother wishing some of the Chicks to pay you a visit later on. I hope they will be able to do so, if it does not put you out.

I have not seen Regy's[2] photo but hear it is good, he promised to have quite as good looks as the others, if not superior.

---

[1] Budleigh Salterton - a pretty East Devon coastal town approximately 15 miles from Exeter and on the mouth of the River Otter.
[2] Reginald Winnington Fanshawe – 3rd son of TBF, born at Bath in 1871.

I cannot account for the deaths in the Reg't having occurred among people of a certain age instead of younger, unless that the former drank more than the latter. When I say drank, I do not mean they did so in excess in the least but merely took their beer <u>in the middle of the day</u> instead of waiting till the sun went down.

I cannot say I do understand from John about the money – as I have not the slightest idea if I get anything from Aunt C but I will not bother you about it. When I had the money for my Majority, John found it - to make a long story short, & I said I would if necessary, pay the interest if required – which he never asked for till now when he put it forward, luckily it does not matter to me in the least. Please do not allude to this in any way to him. I see you are good & kind enough to say in your last that about £320 will come to me some day – I wish you would make use of it yourself.

Minn told me of the arrival of the plate that fell to Helen Mason's[1] share from Aunt C. Pray thank H Mason for her very kind present, with my love. I must ask you also not to say anything to Minnie about John & the interest of the money for the Majority…

I am sorry to hear John is so hard up, it is a pity he does not insist on Evy's doing something, anything better than idling about doing nothing at his age – a clerkship would be better than nothing. Evy would not like it perhaps? Basy[2] will do well when once started…

---

[1] Helen Shaw Lefevre, 1st cousin of TBF, married George Mason at St. George, Hanover Square (1857).
[2] Basil Thomas Fanshawe, 2nd son of John G Fanshawe (1857 - 1944) civil engineer and later tea plater in Ceylon.

I should not have thought that John would have gone to the expense of sending Bab & Mabel[1] to the drawing room[2] this year if he was so short - but I suppose he knows his own affairs best.

I am sorry to hear that Dick was again suffering from 'climatisation' when he last wrote & that the doctor at Canterbury[3] does not give him much hope of his leg getting quite sound. His cottage & garden seems to be doing well & the cottage improved with the furniture he mentions as having got into it. I trust his prospects of getting on the line surveying[4] this year may come off. Am glad the book on surveying sent over has proved useful. I am afraid from what you say that the Russell's prospect about buying land at the Cape & getting Dick to superintend will fall through. I do not think Russell ought to have suggested the place without having well thought it over, and having once proposed it, should have stuck to it – at any rate given a trial to Dick. The land has got to be bought, & when it is & the advantages & disadvantages found out, a decision could be reached at. I doubt Dick being tempted by the offer.

It must have been pleasant having Helen so close to you at Smith Dorrien's, though I do not suppose you met very often. How is Col. Smith Dorrien[5]?

---

[1] Beaujolois Mabel Fanshawe (1859 – 1940), elder daughter of John G Fanshawe and TBF's niece.

[2] 'The Drawing Room' - a formal afternoon function when ladies were presented as 'debutantes' to the Royal Court of Queen Victoria.

[3] Richard 'Dick' Fanshawe migrated to New Zealand 1861, he returned to England for a visit in 1878 then returned to his home at Southbridge, Canterbury N.Z where he died in 1902.

[4] In 1876 the Department of Lands & Survey in New Zealand was being set up preceding the founding of the New Zealand Institute of Surveyors.

[5] Robert Algernon Smith Dorrien of Haresfoot, Berkhampstead, Herts. Captain 3rd Light Dragoons and 16th Lancers, Colonel Herts Militia (1814 – 1879). Mary Ann Smith Dorrien, his wife (1825 – 1909).

I hope Ned will do well on his cruise[1] & Joe find his prospects brighter than he anticipated over in America when once started to work. I see the 100th Reg't are under orders for India in this next cold weather. I wonder where Charlie will go & how he will like the gorgeous East!

I have not heard from John since March 31st & I wrote on May 20th. Helen wrote on April 10th & I wrote on May 6th since which I have not heard from either. I suppose the London season[2] was too busy for them to find time.

How is H Lefevre & how does his nose look, better or worse? My love to him when you meet!

I am afraid Selina[3] will have no chance of finding a tenant for her house, everyone is wanting to let not to hire.

I believe we shall find the Royal Commission is a great sell, after all does nothing for anyone. I shall become December next, 48 or in my 48th year, so I have 7 years to obtain the rank of General & am now only a Lt. Colonel & if you take up an army list you will see the list I have to get through of Colonels before I should come near to being a General, and then lose all the money I paid. No thank you! After 31 years' service I think I may fairly give up knocking about, do not you? At any rate I intend, if I live to do so, I shall hang on if my health lasts till March or April next, come home & then either sell or retire on full pay. I have nothing to wait for…

---

[1] Edward Fanshawe Denison applied for a British passport in 1874.
[2] In the nineteenth century the most active part of the London season was the period between Easter and when parliament adjourned for the summer months of July or August.
[3] Selina Gostling lived a 29 Park Street, Bath – 1861 Census.

What a dreadful accident on board the Thunderer[1] & the papers seem to hint at gross neglect on someone's part. How shocking to think of so many people being sent out of this world by someone's fault!

Mrs Bravo's case[2] seems a funny one, her [xxxxx} deaths are bad - father & grandfather deviants & mother & grandmother very bad so suppose it was in the family.

We have been doing less than usual of late for the racquet court has been shut up for repairs for couple of weeks, much to my regret, but it opened again yesterday. I have been doing long walks by myself as I could not ride having rubbed the skin off my knee one day when on duty.

I have been planting some cucumber seeds that Minnie sent me out. I put them in the ground on a Saturday and they were well up on the Wednesday following – quick work in the open air, is it not?

I have dined out once or twice lately but there is not much going on.

I lost one of my Majors on the 14th of last month. Major Weeding who died from Cholera at a place called Ahmedabad, some hundreds of miles from here in the Bombay Presidency, where he had gone on leave. Taken ill on 12th July & dead on the 14th - one does not get much notice in this country! He was a good officer, but not a man I could make a friend of, poor fellow. I am very sorry & shocked at his end & am afraid it will not calm Minnie's feelings

---

[1] The Royal Navy's '*Thunderer*' suffered a disastrous explosion on 14 July 1876 when 45 people were killed due to a boiler bursting as the ship left Portsmouth harbour. The cause was found to be a broken pressure gauge and a corroded safety valve so that when the steam stop valve to the engines closed, the pressure in the boiler rose without being able to escape.

[2] 21st April 1876 - Mrs Florence Bravo's husband Charles died from poisoning by antimony. A notorious case that was never solved but Florence Bravo remained the main suspect.

when she hears of it, though so far away from this. It is not a country to live in unless obliged!

The Reg't is pretty healthy just now & trust we shall have no more sickness. I shall be glad when we get to October & cool weather. My chum Chadwick returns on the 8th of the month. He seems to be enjoying himself up in Kashmir. I am all alone again in my house as Garnett who has been living with me has gone on two months leave to Bengal to see his brother who commands the 11th Hussars.

The mail of July 28th has arrived in Bombay we hear by telegram[1] today – but we shall not get our letters till Thursday.

I will not close this till tomorrow in case I have anything to add. Do not forget our little arrangement about the brougham when you return to town.

So with much love to you, ever dearest Mother

Your most affectionate son

Basil

---

[1] By 1870 telegraph lines connected London with India, enabling home authorities to issue orders based on up to date information.

Letter from Thomas Basil Fanshawe to his mother
Royal Hotel
Poona[1]
Thursday Sept 14th (1876)

My Dearest Mother,

I dare say you will wonder at what I am doing down here but I had a long spell of Kamptee & this month till the middle of next up there, is unpleasant & not particularly healthy. I thought I would take a months' leave & come here for a change as the climate is quite different.

We left Kamptee on Monday evening, slept at Nagpore, 4 miles off where the railway starts from & started on Tuesday morning at 8.30 & got here yesterday afternoon or evening at 6 o'clock. Two beside myself, which made it pleasant travelling as it is a long time to travel 27 hours straight off the reel – it certainly is a different atmosphere & it felt quite cold last night and an absence of punkah is truly delicious – one never sees a punkah pulled here except at messes. This place is very full just now as the races[2] are going on & will be for another ten days during the time they last, every alternate day.

Kamptee will or ought to be getting cold when I return on 12th October. I am on what is called privilege leave, am allowed 60 days in each 12 months which does not interfere with command allowances or pay. I have only taken 30 days or shall have when I return.

---

[1] Poona (Pune) - a large city within the Poona Municipality with a rail line from Bombay that became established in 1858. Towards the end of the nineteenth century, Poona played an important part in social and religious reforms prominent in the struggle for Indian independence.
[2] The first racecourse in India was set up at Madras in 1777 and at Poona the Indian St Leger is run every September.

Has Minnie told you how nearly we, the whole station at Kamptee, were being drowned?

The water in the river rose 46 feet[1] & a few feet more, very few would have been left. Caused by continual heavy rain & the rivers into which the river goes that flows past Kamptee being flooded & damming the water back.

The Artillery Barracks were under water & I had to get our own sick out of hospital on elephants & this over a place I walked over every day to the racquet court, which was now a roaring torrent some 12 feet deep & 150 yards broad & so strong at last, that the elephants refused to face it.

Our Reg't bazaar in which the native followers attached to the Reg't live, was completely flooded & a perfect creek. I rode there the following morning & hardly a house was standing & all the unfortunate natives were houseless & lost everything they possessed.

Luckily there was not much loss of life, the flood begun about 6 o'clock in the morning & continued till about 5.30 that evening (Monday) the 4th & the next morning it had vanished & except for the slime & mud left you would hardly have known there had been such a thing. I do not wish to see another like it – we lost no life, it was all among the natives that loss took place – they would hang on, poor creatures, to their houses & little all & at last the houses went

---

[1] Early in October 1871 several UK regional newspapers carried reports of the flood. Some included extracts from a letter written by another soldier at Kamptee whose information confirms the events much as told by TBF.

The Following is an extract from a private letter, dated Nagpore, Sept. 5:-

'My dear -,

Just a few lines to tell you that there has been a disastrous flood in Kamptee.

It rained all day Sunday, Sunday night, and Monday and the rain would appear to have been very heavy to the westward of Kamptee, as the river had swollen, and the Gora Bazaar washed away. It is reported that about 1500 lives are lost, but this may be over the mark. The bridge near the church is washed away. The flood extended as far as the post office…

I hear since that the post office is down to the ground. Many who were saved have escapes as by a miracle. The families of the soldiers were taken away on elephants. Colonel - went yesterday, but was stopped where the bridge used to be near the church. He then went on to the 'circular drive', but could not get into the station: the water was too deep, so he had to return, and he has gone today"

The writer concludes by remarking that these are only rough reports, and that more precise details will be learnt in a day or two. No doubt the number of lives said to be lost is very large, and probably the actual loss will be less.

Persons acquainted with the Kamptee cantonment

with a crash & buried them in the ruins – a similar flood has not been known since 36 years ago[1].

The two ends of the stations were quite cut off by a stream sweeping through the middle & which could be only be crossed on elephants. What useful sagacious beasts they are, I do not know how we should have got on without them on the occasion.

Now let me thank you for your last of 18th August which reached me this day week. I have now carefully read the warrant or rather the proposals put forth by the Royal Commission & must say I <u>cannot</u> understand them, as far as effects my present or future position or prospects. In fact I believe that I am rather better off under the present rules – the only thing is the widow's pension which if I sell would not be of any use, & then again it may not be carried.

I can retire now with a pound a day being the full pay of my rank & a bonus of nearly £2,000 at least. I believe so, having completed 30 years' service which entitles me to so doing or I could sell out & by so doing should get about £5,000 which includes regulation & over regulation as Major, which rank I held at the abolition of purchases.

---

[1] TBF may have been mistaken by 10 years - probably referring to widespread flooding throughout India, as reported in the London Morning Post and many provincial papers on or about 2 November 1849.

My income would be nearly £200 a year less by selling out than by taking full pay retirement viz:

£1 per days -	£365	
Interest on £1960 at say 5 per cent *(bonus for going)* -	£100	Full Pay
	£465	

5000 pounds realised by selling commission at 5 per cent = £250
Full Pay   £465

Interest of Commission
Money   £250
____

Difference between income   =   £215

But then there would be the 5000 to leave the chicks & if anything happened to me the 365 pounds goes – so it is rather a hard matter to decide.

I have tried to put it before you as clearly as I can. I do not see the fun of working on for the same amount as I can get for retiring & doing nothing, and as I have said before, I must go sooner or later as I never would become a general.

So I think if Minn & Mr Gosselin like the idea, next March or April will see me en route home, if all goes well, on leave. I <u>do not</u> spend another hot season for any consideration at Kamptee, if I can by hook or crook avoid so doing.

Minn & I, neither of us like being separated & if it was not for the rupees I get, which will help in their education, I should send in my papers tomorrow, however I am not going to do anything in a hurry

Lilian Emily Fanshawe at the age of seven - 1876
LBBD Archives at Valence House

Reginald Winnington Fanshawe at the age of five – 1876
LBBD Archives at Valence House

& shall consult Chadwick about these proposals but I am nearly sure that neither of us are any better off than we are at present.

I heard from Chadwick on 1st Sept, he was in a great hurry to get away from Cashmere as cholera was so rampant & all along his road down to Lahore[1]. I sincerely hope that he will reach Kamptee all right about the 8th next month and that I should find him so when I get back. He would have started but his shawls[2] were not ready for him.

Am sorry Lizzy is so ailing, she does not give a brilliant account of herself – I wonder what the cause for she has been so free from those attacks of late.

Both the boys did well at school. Thanks for your congratulations on Gerry's having done so well & got a fringe – he is a sharp little fellow & when one recollects the difference of age between him & Bertie… the latter did well & his best, which is a good thing to know. I do not like Reggy's last photo, the shade on his right cheek or some thing or another makes it look to me swollen & so disfigured it. He seems much grown.

London must look deserted. I daresay you will be glad of a change to Russells. I hope he has better luck this year with his birds. Partridges from all accounts it seems to have been one of the best for years past.

---

[1] Lahore, located in Punjab state is now in Pakistan near the border with India.

[2] Shawls made from fine cashmere wool are generally called Pashmina. The wool is from four breeds of Cashmere goat - Changthangi from Changthang plateau, Malra from Kargil area in Kashmir region, Chegu from Himachal Pradesh in northern India and Pakistan, and Chyangara from Nepal. These fine, soft, warm shawls have been woven and worn for many centuries. More recently they have come back into twenty-first century western fashion.

I hope you have heard again from Dick. I should not be surprised if with the lazy & tiresome journey before him, not so free in his own time, that he would decline the offer at the Cape as he would be to a certain extent answerable for whatever he engaged to look after – but shall be pleased to hear he continues doing well…

I think you might accept my offer about the brougham with little violence to your feelings, but indeed such a slight offer does not need so much acknowledgement dearest Mother. I should be so glad if you would only have one, say only when you go out to dinner – it would be so much, more safe for you.

I do not think the excitement in the Bravo case out here was anything much – you see at a month or 3 weeks lapse in time in conveying the news makes a great difference, I do not think Mrs Bravo a perfect person but I do think the questions she was asked as to former intimacy with Doctor Gully and his antecedents were quite uncalled for as they elucidated no point on the matter before the jury as to how Bravo came by his death.

Ned I hope has meet with a turn of luck with the wrecks – at last he is most persevering. Pity Evy does nothing or can find nothing to turn his hand to.

I did not know that Hope[1] was thinking of leaving Parsloes. I should say he was a shifty gentleman in many ways.

The rupee question is this: there is so much silver now in the market that where, as formerly it could be bought for about (I)5/- an ounce, it now can be bought for (I)4/2 or (I)4/3 which lowers the actual value of the rupee & that with exchange, which I do not understand

---

[1] Tenant of Parsloes Manor – Colonel William Hope (1834 – 1909) Royal Fusiliers awarded VC for action on 18 June 1855 at Sebastopol, Crimea.

or can attempt to explain, only enables you to remit to England at a loss of about 25 per cent.

For instance, if I wanted to remit you a £100, I should have to pay down 1225 rupees which is its value (£100) - at present 1000 rupees is supposed or rather was to be equal £100 – now you have to pay 250 rupees or if I sent you 1000 rupees, you would only receive 750 - the other 250 going to pay for the fall in value in the rupee & rate of exchange. So I lose £25 in every hundred that I remit – a serious loss. I hope it may improve.

I have said my little all so with best love ever dearest Mother,

Your most affectionate son

Basil

(written in pencil)   Turn over

If Robert Carey or anyone can enlighten you in what way I am benefitted by the new proposals, I shall be glad to hear, but I do not see myself. My love to him when you meet!

Letter from Thomas Basil Fanshawe to his mother
Kamptee
Friday Oct 27th (1876)

My Dearest Mother,

The English Mail that arrived here this morning brought me yours of Oct 5th & its enclosure from Dick, herewith returned. Many thanks for both – I am glad to find that Dick is so charmed with the prospect held out to him & hope that nothing will fall out to prevent it becoming as good a thing as it promises. I am quite sure it would not be for want of looking after things that Dick would fail in giving satisfaction or doing justice to the estate with which he was placed in charge.

It was not my fault that my letter did not reach Minnie but some fault of the postal authorities – she says it was between Bombay & England – I imagine the train from Nagpore to Bhusawal (the junction of the line to Calcutta) was late & so missed the steamer. I regret very much the anxiety she was caused by it. I trust it will not happen again.

I wrote to you from Poona, as well as on my return here, so you will be pretty well up in my movements & of Chadwick's return.

I am sorry to find that you were suffering from a bad cold when you wrote but trust it has long since vanished & left no bad effects behind. I am flourishing, trust God - & look forward to every day passed as getting nearer to my getting out of the country - D.V.[1] & once left, if I am spared to do so, nothing would tempt me to come out again – not even to be made Governor General of India! And I am looking forward to the day when I can leave, which will depend greatly on what reply I get from you in answer to my last about my

____

[1] D.V. – *deo volente* (Latin) - 'God Willing'.

debt for my majority & how it can best be settled. However, I will not say anything more on that unpleasant topic – mind I have no wish to repudiate in any way the advantage of the money that enabled me to obtain the majority[1] – but I do say that I think it was treating me hardly to let it come out to such an amount without letting me know what was hanging over my head.

Am glad to hear that Mrs Russell is looking so well, Russell[2] seems to have little sport & not to be over keen on what little there is – he seems to get worse & worse about making a start - who shoots with him now, anyone - or does he roam out by himself? The amount of capital he means to invest does not seem large, Chadwick who has been there (the Cape) thinks that he would get about 600 acres for that sum – unless for sugar planting, when he would of course get less than what I have named. I hope it will prove a prosperous investment for both him & Dick.

Am glad Wallace was so flourishing, he was in the Reg't several years with me.

Helen's letter has not yet reached – I suppose to save the extra two pence or 4d via Brindisi, she sent it via Southampton – just makes a week or 10 days difference in getting the letter – so till it arrives I am in ignorance of her proceedings, beyond her being at Scilly[3].

---

[1] Purchase of commission eleven years previously – April 1865.
[2] Colonel Champion Russell, a keen naturalist, wildfowler and friend of 'fisherman gunners' was well known on the Blackwater estuary in Essex where he kept a large punt gun. A prolific writer of letters to 'The Times', 'The Field' and 'Essex Chronicle' concerning wildfowl, he advocated and successfully achieved a recognised closed season for shooting of all protected animals.
[3] Helen Denison probably stayed at Tresco Abbey the home of Lt Thomas Algernon Smith-Dorrien-Smith (1846 – 1918) - he had succeeded his uncle in 1871 to become Lord Proprietor of the Isles of Scilly and is credited with introducing the successful industry of producing and exporting flowers from the islands.

Am sorry to hear of Ned having had such bad luck with his venture this summer.

I wonder Charlotte Branfill[1] never having changed her name – is it too late for her to do so now?

My watch goes uncommonly well & is first rate. I had an accident with it within a week of landing at a place called Igatpuri[2], it slipped out of my uniform coat on the flags of the station (railway), wonderfully to say the clasp was not broken nor the case damaged but a pin inside got bent & I had to send it down to Bombay to one of our fellows who had to remain behind with some women & children of the Reg't & he got it repaired, since which it has gone capitally! Many thanks to you all for giving me such a useful present, am glad our little present to you keeps such good time. I only wish it was more worth your acceptance…

We get the telegrams daily, about two days later news than you have than at home. For instance in the Pioneer (a Bengal paper)[3] of yesterday 26th, we have news from England of the 24th October but I see there is to be a session of Parliament on 12th December[4] – I suppose it all depends upon Russia if there is to be a general row in Europe or not. England at present seems to wish to steer clear of the business – I am afraid the small number of troops we could put on

---

[1] Charlotte Branfill of Upminster Hall was then 44 years old. In 1885 she married Arthur Richard Dodson who died in 1905 but Charlotte lived until the age of 90, dying in 1922.

[2] Igatpuri a town and hill station in Nashik District in the state of Maharashtra, located in the Western Ghats. The town is still a major railway centre.

[3] The Pioneer Mail, printed in English and published in Allahabad began as a weekly in 1865. By TBF's time it had evolved into a daily paper with Alfred Sinnett as Editor. From 1887 to 1889 an assistant editor on the paper was Rudyard Kipling.

[4] The political/religious conflict between Russia & Turkey that threatened the peace gained in Eastern Europe as a result of the Crimean War – often referred to as 'the Eastern Question'.

the field, could be a very small handful – no comparison with Continental armies who count their 7 or 800 [horses] and fighting men.

Saturday Oct 28. – I got as far as this last night before mess & I must finish if this is to go by the mail today.

I have not been playing racquets much for the last 10 days till this week, as the balls were so bad it was no fun playing with them, but a fresh supply arrived this week so I have been a regular attendant again.

I had a quiet dinner with the General, only 8 or us last Monday, and that is about all the dissipation I have had of late.

We are starting a Reg't 'At Home' from 4.45 to 7 every alternative Wednesday - Lawn Tennis[1] & Badminton for the ladies of the station. I think it a very slow affair, & stupid unless one plays oneself, but all the other messes have it – so I suppose we must.

We have started a theatrical[2] troop & they give their first performance next Wednesday. I hope it will go off well – it is a good thing for those men of the Reg't who have a turn that way, as it is employment & keeps them out of worse amusements.

Our nights & mornings are very pleasant & I find a blanket all night very comfortable but I sleep with all the doors & windows open & do not suppose I shall shut them for another 3 weeks.

---

[1] Lawn Tennis had only recently been invented as a recreation to be played out of door on grass by Major Walter Wingfield. The equipment was first sold as a boxed set in 1873 and the new activity became instantly popular with the younger members of the British upper classes.

[2] Army Theatricals were popular in colonial British India, helping to establish the strong theatrical traditions remaining in India today.

I am very busy just now, as we have a new drill to learn & teach the Reg't & this is the busiest time of the year with us, the cold season as it is called, but it is hot enough in the middle of the day.

I think I have told you what little I have to get down. I wish it was more amusing to peruse.

So with best love,

Ever dearest Mother,

Your most affectionate son

Basil

I recollect the Francis's very well – one of the daughters if I mistake not, married a man of the 50th Reg't & was at Colchester[1] with us. Lived a few doors higher up than we did & her brother came down to stay with her. He is a great cricketer & very good. Robinson, I think was her husband's name – in the 50th.

I wonder how Milly[2] & his wife[3] will like coming out to this country? Most people, unless very young, soon get disenchanted with India & Indian life. I wish there was some shooting to be got from this place, Chadwick & another of ours were out on Thursday last & their bag - one teal[4]! Not much inducement to try, is there?

---

[1] Presumably between September 1871 and September 1873 – the 'Duke of Wellington's Regiment Locations List' shows this as the only period when the regiment was stationed at Colchester.
[2] Major Æmelius De Vic Tupper (1836 – 1895) Royal Artillery retired Lt. Colonel (1886), son of Anna Maria Le Marchant & Daniel Tupper & 1st cousin to TBF.
[3] Eliza Jane Park married 1865.
[4] Small ducks with bright green wing patches.

Once more, Goodbye.

Would you kindly ask Robert Carey when you see him, if a man taking a full pay retirement, can after being on full pay a certain number of years, *commute[1] his full pay for a sum down?

*say two or three years.

---

[1] To give up part or all of a pension payable from retirement in exchange for an immediate cash sum.

Letter from Thomas Basil Fanshawe to his mother
Kamptee
Friday Nov 17th (1876)

My Dearest Mother,

Although the mail does not depart till tomorrow I will begin my scrawl today by thanking you for your last long letter of October 20th which reached me on Sunday, though it came on the Friday – but I was out in the jungle for 3 days with Col. Chadwick & Capt. Nesbitt[1].

We left this on Thursday afternoon, shot Friday & Saturday & returned on the Sunday – we had little or no sport though we went over a deal of ground and the total bag between the 3 of us was only 10 couple of snipe, two or three duck and a partridge. What one would have thought an indifferent bag for a morning's work for one gun in former days at places I have been at. I shall not try the shooting again it is not worth the trouble.

We had a very jolly time though & were very comfortable. We have had such lots of experience that it would have been our own fault had it been otherwise. The country was nothing worth seeing, chiefly grain fields – or jungle.

Now let me congratulate you on having obtained your 81st year[2] & may you have many more! There are not many people at your time of life that can do what you do & always enjoy to assist anyone in any way, instead of having people to assist you. Long may you continue so dearest Mother - & thanks for all your prayers & good

---

[1] Capt. Edward Nesbitt, 33rd Regiment, enlisted as ensign 1865 (1901 Census: lists as 'Colonel in the Army').

[2] At the heading of the original letter a pencil note has been made (author unknown) *1876 – a mistake in speaking of his mother having attained 81st*.

wishes for me & Minnie - I should have much liked to have been of your family party at John's…

I do hope with you, that the Russell's projected scheme for giving Dick a helping hand at the Cape, may come off all right. I am sure Dick would do his best for both Russell & himself.

The telegrams we see in the papers (local dailies) are very warlike. I suppose no one knows how it will all end – no doubt all the young men in the army are hoping for a general row[1] & foreign service, in the hopes of promotion. I do not suppose there is much chance of our (33rd) being sent if anything does take place – we are so far away from the scene of action & in the centre of India – and if troops do go from India I imagine that Sikhs[2] & Ghurkas[3] will be the ones selected.

Gov't would never be foolish enough to commit the same folly of devoiding this country of English troops, after the lesson of 1857[4] - goodbye to all the Royal Commission proposals on retirement, if there is a war!

I myself cannot see why I should not settle down quietly & get as much or more for doing nothing than I should for remaining on. I think I have fully earned rest, and as I have no future professional

---

[1] The prelude to the Russo-Turkish War (1877–1878) - causing most of the Ottoman Empire to be liberated by the Russians. As a consequence, the Balkans were to remain under Russian influence which caused alarm to Britain France and Germany. The Congress of Berlin opened in an attempt to reach agreement in regard to alliances and influence in the region.

[2] Followers of Sikhism, the Sikhs had been loyal to the British during the Indian Mutiny of 1857 and remained trusted and loyal.

[3] The Ghurka Regiments remained loyal during the Indian Mutiny. They later served in Burma, Afghanistan, the North-East and North-West Frontiers of India, Malta and in the Russo-Turkish War of 1877–78. 'The Ghurkas' became highly esteemed for their loyalty, bravery and professionalism.

[4] The Sepoy/Indian Mutiny.

prospect, bar a depot centre which is not in my line at all, I do not see why I should endure being separated from wife & children longer than I can help. I think I could do nothing, as well as most people, perhaps better. However there is no great hurry & with the prospect of a row billowing, I could not well leave till it is settle one way or other.

I see the Turks are sending a fleet of ironclads[1] into the Black Sea which I imagine is as near meaning war as anything can do…

We (33rd) are armed with the Martini-Henry rifle which very few Reg'ts in India are, except those who came out last year. So if a force goes to Egypt[2] there is just a chance we may be ordered there – but please do not let Minnie know until it is "un fait accompli".

Gaspard & Milly Tupper I presume will soon be in Bombay as their ship the 'Jumna' which brought us out, is just due. I wonder how Milly and his wife will like India?

Chadwick and I had our bungalow photographed a few mornings back but I have not yet got the photos printed, only one as a specimen. I will ask Minnie to send you one of those I send her. I am sending her by this mail a photo of the officers of the Reg't taken a fortnight back. I do not suppose, except myself there is one you recollect. I will tell her to send you a copy & if you care for it – you had better keep it.

---

[1] Steam-propelled warships protected by iron or steel armour plates were used from approximately 1860. The iron cladding was a response to the vulnerability of wooden warships easily destroyed by explosive or incendiary shells.
[2] Egypt was greatly in debt and had food shortages, floods and famine. Egyptian Nationalism was on the rise causing the British Prime Minister Disraeli to react quickly. By paying off some of the debts Britain was able to secure substantially more shares in the Suez Canal from the Egyptian Government, although for many years after, problems persisted in the region.

Am glad to hear John & his belongings & Helen are looking so well for the country air. Helen's letter has not yet reached me, perhaps it may tomorrow & if it does I will let you know. I have always heard Scilly & Tresco Abbey described as being very perfect in their way – the drawback being getting there & once there, getting away again but one cannot have everything in this world – it is to be hoped we may in the next…

I sincerely trust Col. Smith Dorrien will be all the better for his fit of the gout[1] which though not pleasant if when it departs leaves him free from other complaints he will have cause to be thankful for the visitation. I am sorry he has had such poor luck with his dressing – I hear on all sides it is very difficult to get anything to do.

John, I should think would rather enjoy a visit to Paris at Sir R Burdett's[2] expense – for I should otherwise decline the kind offer…

I hope Selina and her daughter[3] will reap all the benefit they anticipate from a winter at Malta.

---

[1] Painful inflammation of joints, usually in the toes, ankles or knees when the joint feels hot and tender and the skin becomes very red. Caused by an accumulation of uric acid in the blood, Gout was usually treated by an application of an ice pack; today non-steroid anti-inflammatory drugs are used.

[2] Sir Robert Burdett of Bramcote, 6th Baronet (1796 -1880) - only son of the reformer politician Francis Burdett and Sophia Coutts, daughter of the banker Thomas Coutts. He served as Sheriff of Derbyshire in 1848 and died unmarried in 1880. His sister was the philanthropist Angela Burdett-Coutts, 1st Baroness Burdett-Coutts reputed to be the wealthiest woman in England when she inherited her banker grandfather's fortune of £1.8 million pounds in 1837.

[3] Selina Gostling, aged 21 living with her widowed mother, also Selina, at 29 Park Street, Bath - next door to TBF's family and his parents-in-law Mr & Mrs Gosselin. All three families were related via Guernsey origins.

I should think they would find the place lively enough, though expensive with the Duke & Duchess of Edinbro'[1] there, and if this row takes place all the troops & ships that will be collected together there prior to their final destination – whatever that may be.

I hope Eliza Le Marchant[2] will find the change to London do her good & escape the cold of the winter there which she so much dislikes – I have not heard from Edward Le M't in the 67th for some time & as I am the culprit in not replying to his last letter. There is so little to write about from this dull place.

Mr Mihill[3] must have been very pleased to have met you at the Romford Station[4] – am glad they put a good man as a vicar[5] at

---

[1] Duke and Duchess of Edinburgh – Queen Victoria's second son Prince Alfred (1844 – 1900) and his wife the Grand Duchess Maria Alexandrovna of Russia were married January 1874. The Prince, who enlisted in the Royal Navy as an ensign in 1858 had a long naval career and became the most travelled of any previous member of the British royal family. Malta was his home station for several years and his third child, Princess Victoria Melita was born on 25th November 1876 – one week after this letter.

[2] Eliza Le Marchant –1st cousin of TBF and sister of Gaspard & 'Milly' Tupper. A mutual distant cousin Robert Le Marchant, Rector of Little Rissington became her husband but Guernsey born Eliza disliked the rural life of her husband's Cotswold rectory and suffered many bouts of poor health. Despite this the couple had 9 daughters & 6 sons including Edward Le Marchant, mentioned here as serving in the 67th Regiment.

[3] Dagenham Farmer, William Mihill was resident in Dagenham Parish where TBF's late father had been the Vicar for 40 years. Several generations of the Mihill family had farmed 120 acres at Grove Farm and would have been well acquainted with Mrs Fanshawe.

[4] The Essex market town of Romford lies approximately 2 miles from Dagenham and the station opened in 1839 as the eastern terminus of the Eastern Counties Railway from Mile End.

[5] During 1876 a new Vicar, the Revd John J S More was inducted into the Parish of St. Peter and St Paul and he became well respected and long serving.

Gerard Lewis Fanshawe at the age of ten - 1876
LBBD Archives at Valence House

Herbert Cecil Fanshawe at the age of nine – 1876
LBBD Archives at Valence House

Dagenham at last. I did not know there had been a change but I should think any would be an improvement on the last[1].

Anderson[2], poor man seems in a bad way – he must be a certain age now for I can recollect him as no chicken.

It must be a satisfaction to the Russells to hear that Edith liked what she had seen of the Cape – Chadwick who has been stationed there a good deal, says it is not a place to make much money, but a man can live in clover on his farm – which sounds well for Dick's prospects. I hope the Russells will like the place selected for them, how many children has Mrs Russell now?

Aunt Margaret[3] seems quite to have adopted a foreign life in France, I suppose she likes it or would not remain. I am afraid Seymour will do no good & from what I hear is rather a dissipated young scamp but please do not repeat. What does Johnny do with himself, anything?

Never fancy, dear Mother your letters are too long or that I find them dull – I am always delighted to receive them or any from home. Minnie in her last gives good account of herself & the children, the boys seem to be doing well at their school which is satisfactory. Lizzy seems improving on the whole which am glad of. She sent me two capital photos of the two boys. I suppose you have seen them, done by a new process. Bertie seems to me the most grown – both promise to be good looking!

---

[1] Revd John Farmer - previous incumbent of the parish from 1861 to 1876.
[2] Alexander Anderson (1808–1890) of Wallace Lodge, Romford Road, Chadwell Heath, Dagenham was a well-respected farmer with substantial additional land investments in many areas around Dagenham Village and Parsloes Manor.
[3] Lady Margaret Le Marchant (née Taylor) died at Folkestone in 1903. Sister in law of TBF's mother, she was the widow of Lt. Gen. Sir John Gaspard Le Marchant KCB, GCMG - former Governor of Malta who died in 1874.

Mrs Gosselin, I conclude you know, has been laid up with a sprained ankle – caught her foot in the last stair going down from the drawing room – they are nasty tedious things [*inserted above*] sprains, to get perfectly right again.

We rub on here in our usual routine, duty & racquets – I believe there are to be one or two dinner parties and a dance next week, people begin to wake up a bit in the so called cold weather. The nights & mornings are very cool & the mornings quite sharp. I am glad of two blankets over me at night, though I still have open doors & windows – if we could only have this climate all the year, I would not complain, but it is the months of April, May & June that are so trying.

I saw Sir H Foulis[1] death in the papers a short time back, who does his money go to – the hospital, for he had no very near relatives had he? But, I may be wrong.

My watch says it is time for me to dress for mess, so I will finish tomorrow & see what news the mail brings me. Pray excuse the blots in the first sheet, it was the fault of the blotting paper which in this climate seems to lose most of its power in absorbing ink.

Saturday Nov 18th - The English mail arrived this morning bringing me a letter from Minnie & one from a Capt. in our Reg't who is coming out – in fact is now on his way. He is due in Bombay on 6th December.

All flourishing at home except Mrs Gosselin who is now feeling the other leg, which I suppose she must have hurt when she sprained

---

[1] The Revd, Sir Henry Foulis, 9th Baronet Ingleby, was the Prebentary of Lincoln Cathedral and committee chairman and wealthy benefactor to The Brompton Hospital, London. Born in 1800, he died on 7th October 1876 at Ampthill House, Bedfordshire, leaving no descendants. Probate of his estate was granted to a niece & nephew for a sum not exceeding £80,000.

her other ankle and did not feel at the time. The boys seem very eager for school still & bustle off in a great hurry every morning.

Minnie says that the weather has quite changed & feels just like winter. I suppose you do not perceive the cold so much in town.

It was quite sharp & pleasant this morning at ¼ to 7 – rather late for me to be out as a rule, but there is no parade on Saturday.

With love to Helen & John & all their belongings & same to self.

I am dearest Mother, your most affectionate son

Basil

Letter from Thomas Basil Fanshawe to his mother
Kamptee
Dec 9th (1876)

My Dearest Mother,

I have two of yours to answer, one of Nov. 10th which reached me this day week & one of Nov. 17th which came yesterday, a day earlier than usual. My best thanks for both.

I am afraid in this dull place, that I can find little to interest you – no return for your long & most pleasant letters. This ought to reach you about the beginning of the New Year – my best wishes for health & happiness for the coming year & all good wishes of the season and the same to John & his belongings & Helen. The latter wrote to me yesterday or rather I received her last of Nov.~~14~~ 11th yesterday. Pray thank her for it as I am afraid I shall not have time to do so today, & this is the latest mail day.

I was very sorry to find by yours of Nov. 10th that Mabel & Bab had been seedy & John also & that you when you were writing your last, was also a sufferer from and of, your bad colds – but which I trust has long since departed & that you are all right again & able to get about as usual.

You seem to have had a very smart touch of early winter weather, which I hear from Minnie has since vanished. Our weather is most charming now as I think I told you in my last, the mornings & evenings quite sharp. I have had to shut half of my bedroom doors at night & find two blankets very pleasant. I only wish we could have it like this all the year – there would be nothing to complain of in the way of climate. The sun of course, is still hot in the daytime but that one always expects in this country. We shall or ought to have this weather till March.

We have just completed one full year at Kamptee having arrived on the 6th of last December here. I cannot say I have found the time pass quickly. I hope I may find that for the rest of my stay out here it will go quicker.

I am not very grey!!! yet, but on the turn - recollect that last Sunday the 3rd, I began my 48th year. One must begin to show signs of the time but I am wonderfully well & have been, considering all things and the knocking about I have had in all parts of the world. Chadwick is just grey in the beard, you will see him in the photographs we had taken of the Reg't, or rather of the officers & which I asked Minnie to let you see - as well as one of our bungalow, which I do not think much of.

Chadwick has told me he means to quit the service in March or rather leave this mess – I, as well as all the Reg't will be sorry at his leaving. I suppose Campbell[1] will get the majority…

You say Helen is getting streaked[2] - she writes in capital spirits & am glad you are able to report she is looking so well.

I do hope & trust your fears about Dick not going to the Cape will prove groundless, it would be such a disappointment to him. The war[3] cannot last forever & I should think now would be a good time to buy land as it would be less in price. Is the ground or farm that Russell thought of investing in near the seat of the war? Pray do not hesitate to let me know what would be a useful contribution to his (Dick's) outfit if it comes off all right, which I devoutly trust it may!

---

[1]Captain John Henry Campbell of the 33rd Regiment was promoted to Brevet Major 1st October 1877.

[2] 'Streaked' – presumably another reference to greying hair – Helen had just passed her 50th birthday.

[3] Presumably TBF alludes to the conflict in Southern Africa leading to the Anglo-Zulu War of 1879.

It is most kind of you dearest Mother wishing to have the children up or rather some of them after – I hope they will be no trouble to you if they do come & Minnie will I hope take them up. She gives a good account of them all & the boys still like school. She tells me Mrs Gosselin's leg & ankle are a little better but she has now a bad cold & cough. Lizzy is also able to do more than she used – so it looks as if she was on the mend. I suppose the holidays will commence in another week or fortnight, which I hope they will fully enjoy.

I trust John had good sport with Sam Smith[1] shooting – what an infliction it must have been to have had Sir R Burdett to dine & remain till 2.30! I suppose his carriage waiting outside all the time, pleasant for the coachman to have to wait from 10 till past 2 – luckily it does not come often.

'Am sorry to find that Theodore[2] is so unwell, poor man! He certainly is one of the unlucky ones…

I suppose soon we shall know whether Russia & Turkey mean to fight – if they do England would no doubt at once send troops to Constantinople. Charlie Denison hoping no doubt that his Reg't may form part of the forces. I am glad to hear he likes his life & getting on well. I wish Ned had found something to do – perhaps this coming year may prove the lucky one. Joe, Helen tells me is beginning to like his work[3].

---

[1] Probably, Samuel G. Smith (1822 – 1900) who lived at Salcombe Park, Ware, Hertfordshire - partner in his family's private bank - Smith, Payne & Smith, he supported Disraeli's policies and was the Conservative M.P for Aylesbury from 1859 to 1880.

[2] Dr Theodore Boisragon, physician surgeon (1809 – 1881) – 1st cousin of TBF and son of Mrs Mary Annetta Boisragon, only sister of the Revd. Thomas Lewis Fanshawe.

[3] Joseph Basil Denison became a Civil Engineer.

I had a line from our General here yesterday & he had heard from home that gov't felt very little disposed to carry out the recommendations of the Royal Commission - & if there is a war, the whole thing will be shelved for a long time, if not forever. It will make very little difference to me if they do or do not - I gain nothing from the new proposals.

I suppose you have seen the two photos of the boys which I think very good. You will find them much grown since you last saw them.

Emma Le Mat[1] will, I hope like her stay in Guernsey with Caro De Lancy[2].

Gaspard & Milly Tupper with their wives safely arrived in Bombay about a fortnight ago in the 'Jumna', the ship which brought us out. I suppose they have reached their destination which I hear is Amballa[3] by this. Frank[4] I hear, is on his way home. I never expected Mrs Mary, Gaspard's wife, would venture out to this country – I wonder how they will like it?

I had not heard that Mr Hope had been engaged in law about his sewage works, he seems to have made a biggish haul. I suppose he will not leave Parsloes, though he talks about so doing & one might not be able to find a fresh tenant at once, if he did leave. Sorry to hear Anderson is so bad from paralysis.

---

[1] Emma Le Marchant, a daughter of Eliza Tupper & Robert Le Marchant – TBF's 1st cousin once removed.

[2] Caroline De Lancey (1805 -1894) unmarried relative of a Guernsey family connection (probate granted to Capt. Carey De Lancey Gostling).

[3] Ambala separates the rivers Ganges and Indus on the Punjab border. It is surrounded by the River Ghaggarto to the north and River Tangri to the south.

[4] Francis Gerard St G Tupper. – Son of Anna-Maria Le Marchant and Daniel Tupper of St Peter's Port, Guernsey was a 1st cousin of TBF – he was Clerk in the House of Commons.

I have no Reg't news to give you. I take my usual exercise at racquets daily & that and duty are about all. I have dined out twice of late, once at a big feed a fortnight back, given by the officers of the 2nd Light Cavalry[1] to their Colonel[2] on his leaving the Reg't and a dance afterwards – and the next night I dined with Roberts[3], the Quartermaster General here & that is about all.

There is a bachelors' dance next Wednesday & there will be nearly 10 unmarried young ladies present, a most extraordinary number, particularly for Kamptee.

I am asked to dine with the General on Xmas day. The 'at homes' go on as usual, very stupid affairs I think. The Reg'tl theatre is in full blow again & gives 3 performances - tonight, Monday & Wednesday - I think.

Must close, having come to the end of my story which is dull & uninteresting enough I am afraid.

There are to be great doings here on the first for proclamation of the Empress[4]. I am afraid I shall have all the mess drunk for a week – they, the Municipality[5] give the men a dinner & than afterwards sports with money prizes to last for three days – and a day's pay to each man. So they will not know what to do with all the money that

---

[1] 2nd Light Cavalry - officially named the 2nd Dragoons (Royal Scots Greys) in 1877.
[2] Colonel Chaplin.
[3] Frederick Sleigh Roberts, 1st Earl Roberts (1832 – 1914) one of the most outstanding soldiers of the nineteenth century, rose to the rank of Field Marshal and became Commander in Chief of the British Forces (1900-1905). Born into a successful military family, he joined the Bengal Artillery in 1851 and was awarded the VC for action in the India Mutiny (1858). He also served in Abyssinia and all the major campaigns of the late Victorian period.
[4] Proclamation at Delhi of Queen Victoria as Empress of India on 1st January 1877 at the Delhi Durbar (Court)– attended by 1st Earl of Lytton, Viceroy of India and the Maharajas & Nawabs.
[5] The Municipal Council of Kamptee.

Field Marshal Frederick Sleigh Roberts, 1st Earl Roberts,
VC, KG (1832 –1914)
Photograph: Studio of Lock & Whitfield, Regent Street, London

India Kamptee Officers 1878

Duke of Wellington's Regiment Trustees

will be heaped upon them. One way or another a British soldier seldom has any other idea of spending his money except on drink. Of course we have a big parade, fire 102 guns & all that sort of thing.

Now good bye and with the best wishes of the season & for the coming year – to John, Bab, Helen & all their belongings not forgetting yourself,

Ever dearest Mother, your most affectionate son

Basil

Letter from Thomas Basil Fanshawe to his mother
Kamptee
January 6th (1877)

My Dearest Mother,

Thanks many for yours of Dec 15th which reached me this morning & for the reply R. Carey gave to my question you were good enough to ask him for me - & many thanks for his kind offer of answering anything I want to know. Sorry to hear he has not been well. His eldest boy will I hope get thro' his examination[1] all right, his papers seem satisfactory, that he has done.

I have not been out into the jungle again, it really is not worthwhile – no one has done much & very few go out except as a change.

I dined with the General on Xmas day, a party of 19 – I thought of you all at home & wondered who you were dining with – Helen or John? Minnie & chicks were to dine at 28 so Lizzy wrote me word today. I hope they enjoyed their dinner.

We had a grand parade here on Monday last, the 1st – for the proclamation of the Queen as Empress of India. Fired a feu de joie[2] & 101 guns but as we had to parade at ¼ to 11 & did not get back till 1.30 we were very glad when it was over. The General gave a dance in honour of the occasion at night which was kept up till about 3.30. I got home about one o'clock. There had been sports for the men of all ranks & money prizes on Tuesday, Thursday & today – Chadwick who is President of the committee superintending the games will be glad when his labours are over.

---

[1]The Cardwell Reforms 1868 – 1881, no longer permitted the 'purchase' of commission. Entrance to the Army as a commissioned officer required the successful completion of an examination.
[2] French meaning "fire of joy" - a rifle salute used on very rare occasions of national celebration – soldiers fire running shots into the air in rapid succession.

The affair at Dehli for the proclamation[1] must have been worth seeing, the papers are full of nothing else. I suppose Gaspard & Milly Tupper were both there. Except this little excitement, Kamptee has plodded on its usual routine since I wrote you last...

There are some three days racings here about the 22nd & the Reg't is going to give a dance about the end of the month. I told the officers I did not think it necessary but they all seemed to wish it, so I said all right. I suppose we shall have our inspection coming off next month & shall be glad when it is over as there is such a heap of writing connected with the inspection, otherwise I do not mind when the General comes to look at us – I make no difference.

So you think the photo of the officers good - Minnie does not. I wonder what you will think of our bungalow? The officer in white, next me in the photo is Capt. Durrant[2]. Chadwick is sitting with his arms crossed next the colours & Clifton[3] the Dr. on his left – who (Clifton) has a wideawake[4] hat on.

The telegrams today seem more peaceful & gives one an idea that England will not interfere between Russia & Turkey but let them fight it out. Russia has no money & if it comes to blows will find

---

[1] 1st January 1877 - Queen Victoria was proclaimed Empress of India in Delhi. Field Marshal Lord Roberts has left the following description of the salute: 'A salute of one hundred and one salvos of artillery was fired, with a feu-de-joie from the long line of troops. This was too much for the elephants. As the feu-de-joie approached nearer and nearer to them, they became more and more alarmed, and at last scampered off, dispersing the crowd in every direction'.

[2] Capt. Frederic William Durrant, 33rd Regiment, retired 1881 as Honorary Lt Colonel.

[3] Surgeon Major Robert Walter Clifton - appointed to the 33rd Regiment, December 1872. Academic publication 'Case of Foreign Substance in the Oesophagus Terminating Fatally' - Published by Houses of Parliament, 1875.

[4] Hat normally associated with Quakers of North America – made from dark coloured felt having a wide brim turning up at the sides. The crown of the hat is usually short and flat and encircled with a broad band.

Turkey quite able to hold her own. The talk here is that we shall send an army from India to hold Egypt. I do not see why myself, with her fleet in the Mediterranean & do not fancy the [Khudise] would be pleased at our doing so. However, I suppose we shall know soon – not much chance of the Reg't having any share in the matter, I imagine.

I am better off under present existing Regulations & Warrants as far as regards retirement, than the proposals made by Royal Commission, if carried out, would be for me. I shall know soon…

Am very sorry dearest Mother to find that your severe cold hangs about you so long & has made you such a prisoner to the house, to say nothing of the discomfort which it usually carries with it. I trust long ere this reaches you that you will have quite recovered from its bad effects.

It is very good of you wishing to have the children up at Easter but pray do not think of it if they will be too much for you. No doubt they will be delighted to accept your kind invite & have a peep at London – which will be quite a novelty to them.

Our weather continues pleasant enough but the days are lengthening which means look out for the hot weather coming on. It is light till near six o'clock.

You seem to have most wretched weather & very trying, the constant changes – a good sharp frost would do the country good after all the floods & rain[1]. I see the telegrams report as having been pretty general all over the Kingdom.

---

[1] 'The Graphic' magazine in January 1877 included a picture of a view from the North Terrace of Windsor Castle looking out towards Eton to the right. A widely flooded area is visible where the River Thames has swollen and caused problems to

I shall be so pleased to hear that the Russell's scheme about the Cape has not fallen thro & that Dick's prospects of going there will become a certainty. It will be a sad disappointment to him should anything prevent Russell carrying out his idea. Am glad John too had a pleasant letter from Dick.

John, I have not heard from since I wrote to him in September. I suppose he is busy & as you do not mention him, conclude he is all right again. Am glad Bab is looking better & feeling so. She was good enough to send a lot of books down to the children for them to choose from – most kind of her! No doubt Minnie has written to thank her & perhaps the children. I heard from May[1] & Lily[2] this day, but as you no doubt hear pretty often, I will not repeat what you have already heard.

I did not know Helen had been seedy & glad she is picking up – she will rejoice at having her drawing rooms[3] done & free from work people. The rooms must look very nice from your account.

I am afraid Charlie will not see Constantinople just at present though very anxious to do so. I suppose if England does not interfere, his Reg't will come out to this charming climate at the end of the year…

John was lucky to escape going to Paris with Sir R Coutts[1]. The spring would be a much more pleasant time of year to cross the water & for the journey.

---

the Great Western Railway line. These floods began in December 1876 and lasted well into January 1877.

[1] Helen Maude Fanshawe, born at Bath in 1865 - eldest child of TBF.

[2] Lilian Emily Fanshawe, TBF's younger daughter, born 1869 at Portsea, Island, Hampshire.

[3] Presumably, Helen Denison's London home at 33 Wilton Place, she also had a country residence: Marian Lodge, Little Gaddesden, Berkhamsted, Herts.

I hear Uncle Dan Tupper is a turn better & takes more interest in people & things. I suppose Frank is back again with him now after all his travels. I hear he met Selina at Malta for a day, she seems charmed with the island.

My time warns me to stop - so with much love & hoping to hear good accounts of you this next mail, I will bring this uninteresting production to a finish, much to your relief, I imagine. But delays are dangerous & I always like answering by return & keep correspondence down…

Best love to all in Halkin Street & Wilton Place

Ever dearest Mother

Your most affectionate son

Basil

---

[1] TBF refers to Sir Robert Burdett of Bramcote, 6th Baronet (1796 -1880) whose mother was the heiress of Coutts Bank. He served in the Army, retiring as Colonel and was appointed Sheriff of Derbyshire in 1848.

Letter from Thomas Basil Fanshawe to his mother
Kamptee
January 20th (1877)

My Dearest Mother,

Many thanks for your last of Dec. 28th which reached me this morning & all your good wishes for the coming year. I do not think it will be very long now before we meet dearest Mother, for I have sent in my papers to retire on full pay & will tell you why.

I have had a second touch of liver[1]. I had one in the hot weather or rather just before it last year & I had another rather sharper one just before Xmas & from which though much better, still feel & though the Doctor says there is nothing to be alarmed at, at present I still run the risk of having another & worse one, in the hot weather. So I have determined to go while able, instead of leaving my bones out here.

I have never said anything about my former attack to any one, thinking it might be nothing, but this second one quite shook me up, sickness & headache etc.

Please do not tell Minn anything about these bouts. I have merely said I have had an attack of liver & thought it prudent not to run any risk in staying for another hot season & have made as light of it as I could.

I am much better off retiring under present rules & regulations than under the proposed Royal Commission's new scheme. I got £365 a year & a bonus of £2,150 which, full pay, I can commute at any time

---

[1] A commonly used expression relating to general biliousness and possibly jaundice. If Hepatitis followed it would leave a patient vulnerable to serious complications of the liver function.

& <u>between ourselves</u> we can manage nearly £900 a year – no any large sum but I think with care we can manage comfortably.

I propose leaving Bombay about the first week in March in the 'Jumna' but I am not quite certain of the ship & I ought to be home early in April. So after this reaches you, you need not write any more to me here.

I cannot tell you how glad I shall be to get home & see you all again. I am not the least afraid of finding time hang heavy & after 31 years' service I think it time to go. Next year I must have gone anyhow & I do not think running any risk out here compensates for the circumstances. I should certainly have remained in a little longer had it not been for this last go of liver, which is the worst I have ever had! At any rate I felt it more – being older I suppose, one cannot continue as young as one was.

So much for self! - I am glad to find that your cold is all but gone & that you are feeling stronger & better - you must, I am afraid [have] been badly pulled down by it. I shall hope to find you on my return, well & able to get about as well as ever.

Am glad you think the children's letters nice - but not so nice as your presents to them, I expect. Very kind of you, dearest Mother, thinking of them! They seem to have had a happy time at 28 on Xmas day – Mrs Gosselin's leg progresses very slowly, I fear.

So you got the photo of the bungalow – it was taken for the house not for the figures. My house is the white one, Chadwick's the other & neither comes out well. The shape of the trees spoils it.

We have weather something like yours this week – a most heavy thunderstorm on Wednesday night with a deluge of rain – very close, the lightning & continuous peal of thunder for near an hour, between 11 & 12 at night, it woke me! Last night it began to rain about 10 & it lasted till 10 this morning. Most unusual weather for this place & opinions differ as to whether it is a good thing or not. We had nothing like it last year. Some say it will postpone the hot weather, others that it will bring it sooner & that we shall have no more cold weather, which is a pity for we have certainly had a very pleasant cold weather up to this. We shall have the country quite green again after all this rain.

Next week the races here come off – not much to speak of, at least they were not last year & I do not think they will be so good this…

Am glad to hear Helen has shaken off her cold & will I hope, enjoy her visit. Col. Smith Dorrien seems very delicate & not likely to be as sharp as formerly. Am pleased Selina writes so favourably impressed with Malta – it is a place I never liked as a quarter.

Harry[1] must have suffered a good deal from his ears, poor fellow. I can pity him, his quarter Ashlyn's Hall[2] used to be A1 for shooting & fishing but I suppose it is altered like other good quarters.

I do not think Charlie Denison will see much of Constantinople at present. Russia will sneak out of her bluster - she will find Turkey quite enough to fight if she does come to blows & I suppose we shall look on & give her <u>moral support</u>!!! I am afraid even if England did stir in the matter, the 33rd would be one of the last Reg'ts to move to the seat of war. We are in the centre of India & there would be so many Reg't before us to go; that is if they keep the roster.

I do hope that the Russell's idea of a farm at the Cape will come to pass. Poor Dick will be so disappointed should it fall to the ground & trust that Mrs Russell will have told you something decisive in its favour when she came to stay with you. The war there cannot last

---

[1] Lt. Commander Henry Smith Dorrien 1850 – 1931).
[2] Augustus Smith –Dorrien estate at Great Berkhamsted.

forever & this I should imagine would be a first rate time for buying land as it ought to go cheaper.

How unlucky they seem to be at Rissington[1], always something going wrong.

I heard from Gaspard Tupper about a week ago – Mrs Mary & Milly seem charmed with what they have seen of this sunny clime – more than I am…

Robert Carey's son[2] will I hope have passed. What a number of candidates - but the Gov't will never do anything for officers in the way of increasing their pay so long as young men come forward in such numbers. I do hope none of my boys will think of it as a profession. The pay is very little & the amount of work they expect you to give nowadays is very different to what it was when I joined the army & the number of examinations a boy has to pass before being promoted are great, & one has always one to pass. Thank goodness, I never passed one & do not think I have been any the worse officer for not having done so…

Mabel seems to have enjoyed her visit & dance to Bisham Abbey[3] – am glad of it. Wish you had been able to tell me Evy had found something to do & Ned also. The latter seems willing to try anything or everything!

---

[1] Revd Robert Le Marchant family residing at the Rectory, Little Rissington in the Cotswolds.

[2] 2nd Lt. Denis Carey enlisted 1878 - 30th Foot, East Lancashire Regiment.

[3] 'Grand Ball at Bisham Abbey on Thursday 21st instant, G H Vansittart Esq and Mrs Vansittart gave a ball at their historically famous residence, Bisham Abbey. The entertainment, which was carried out with lordly magnificence, was attended by some 300 of the *elite* of this and neighbouring counties. The noble dining room was set apart for dancing, which commenced at ten o'clock to the strains of Edwards' quadrille band. Supper was laid in the magnificent hall of the mansion' *The Bucks Herald – 30 December 1876.* (The Vansittart's had been a military family but by the nineteenth and early twentieth century descendants became prominent politicians).

Hope you will soon be able to get to H Lefevre, in fact will have done so before this reaches you. Give him my love when you meet.

Spring will I trust be a mild one. It is most kind of you wishing to have Minnie & some of the children up at Easter, no doubt they will thoroughly appreciate their visit. Their first, almost I think, to the sights of London – the boys will I trust bring as good a report of their studies from their Master, as they did the previous half.

I had Lily's photo sent me last week. I suppose you have seen it – I like it much & think the young lady promises to be nice looking. I am told she can <u>whistle</u> capitally to May's playing on the piano, a ladylike accomplishment. Minn gives a good account of them.

The Reg't gives a dance next Friday. I suppose I must go, worse luck. I do not care for going out after dinner & there are very few people here that I really like. Chadwick with Fawcett[1] has been out the last three days pig sticking but am sadly afraid all they met with have prevented their riding even if they did find pigs. This is one, if not quite the worse stations for sport I have ever been in, in India.

Chadwick will no doubt succeed me in command but means to go as soon as ever gazetted[2]. He was going this year but as it makes a difference to him of nearly £80 a year going as Major in place of Lt. Col., he wisely waits – though he would rather go. He quite agrees with me that I have done a wise thing in going now instead of waiting for Mr Hardy's ~~proposal~~ warrant if he does bring one out.

I think I have tried your patience enough so in pity will stop.

With best love to all at Halkin Street & Wilton & same to yourself.

---

[1] Captain Rowland Hill Fawcett, 33rd Regiment, enlisted as an ensign May 1858 and retired 1881 with honorary rank of Lt. Colonel – he attended the funeral of TBF.

[2] The publication of an officer appointment or promotion in The London Gazette represents the official public record - established in 1665.

Ever dearest Mother

Yours most affectionate son

Basil

Do dearest Mother put that little arrangement about the brougham whenever you want to go out & do not feel up to a walk, into effect. I mean ordering the brougham & I shall be pleased to think that you are saved fatigue & can settle the bill when I arrive – do please…

Letter from Thomas Basil Fanshawe to his mother
Kamptee
Saturday Feb'y 10th (1877)

My Dearest Mother,

The mail today brought me your last of Jan'y 19th for which many thanks. I was very glad to find that your cold had gone & you were able to get about as formerly. Do be prudent & not try to do too much now that you are right, try & keep so & do not expose yourself by going out in all sorts of weather. And what dreadful weather & floods you seem to have had all over England. It must be the cause of a deal of sickness & misery to the poor people.

So you have been exerting yourself in trying to get a child into one of the asylums & trust you were successful in your endeavours.

I have been better since I last wrote & though able to take my usual exercise, I still feel my side. I had a very rough time of it at Xmas & the first fortnight in January. I never knew what it was to be without pain & as it was the second touch I made up my mind I would not run the risk of another hot season & am quite certain I have done the wisest thing.

They have granted me leave from Simla but I cannot go till I appear in orders or I should lose my passage which I am entitled to, going on full pay. I hope to leave about 13th March in the 'Jumna' which ship I came out in & know the Captain - and if I do leave in her, we ought to arrive about 14th or 15th April – a nice time to get home!

I was looking at the Army List[1] last night & was calculating that after getting my full Colonelcy, if I waited for it next year, I should be about 20 years before I was Major General. When, if I lived so

---

[1] Printed annual army lists (1754-1879) arranged by regiment, of the regular army giving the names of officers with dates of their commissions. Indexed from 1766.

long, I should be about 68 years old & quite fit & ready for any employment, should I not be at that time of life? As for a brigade depot[1] it would not be in my line & I am better off on full pay than I should be at one of those centres & also going now, than under any scheme Mr Hardy may produce, but I doubt if he will any, if he can help it especially as money is wanted & there is supposed to be or will be a deficiency of two million in the revenue at home this year.

I do not say that I shall not be sorry to leave the dear old Reg't I have passed so many long & happy years in, but it must have come next year, whether I liked it or not. Under the five years rule[2] as I see has been put in force in Colonel Chaplin's case[3], 4th Dragoon Guards but I won't run the risk of any more of this vile climate than I can help.

We have had since I wrote last on the 20th January, heavy rains, thunder & lightning. Most unusual at this time of year, but it has made the place quite green again and the weather quite cool, very different to what it was at this time last year. I was quite glad of a blanket this morning early.

The General has not begun his inspections of us yet - in consequence of the effects of the fall from his horse which shook him greatly. But he commences on Wednesday next which (I) am glad of & shall be still more so, when I get all the papers connected with it out of my hands.

---

[1] Brigade headquarters in the UK, which held recruits in training, injured soldiers returning to fitness and officers and men waiting further postings or discharge.
[2] Relating to the official terms of tenure for the rank of colonel.
[3] Frank Chaplin – 4th Royal Dragoon Guards, enlisted May 1846 and promoted to Lt Colonel 1870.

I have been pretty steady at the racquet court except two days this week when I hurt my wrist against the wall & had to stop play – but it is all right now.

Wednesday last was our fortnightly 'At Home' & just after all the people had collected & were playing lawn tennis & badminton, down it came in a bucket & drove every one into the mess where the younger portion consoled themselves by dancing. Luckily the rain did not last very long but it began again about 7.15 & continued till 9 & I thought I should have got a jolly good wetting going round the guards but it stopped at 9.30 & I did my rounds as Field Officer of the day without a drop - it does not look settled weather yet by any means.

Weather-wise, people say that it will make the hot weather both cool & short, a good thing for those who have to remain here.

I believe things are pretty quiet in India itself, but on the frontier by Peshawar[1] things are looking queer with the hill tribes[2] & beyond them again. Turkey seems quite able to hold her own against Russia & seems to have made up her mind to listen to none of the advice prof[f]erred at the conference[3]. So it would seem peace is to be the order of the day, but it must end in a jolly blow up between the two

---

[1] The ancient city of Peshawar is situated in a large valley near the eastern end of the Khyber Pass, close to the modern day Pakistan-Afghanistan border. The region came under British rule when it was captured from the Sikhs in 1849 during the 2nd Anglo-Sikh War.

[2] Karlanris, or "hill tribes," are the third largest group of Pashtuns. They straddle the border areas between Pakistan and Afghanistan in Waziristan, Kurram, Peshawar, Khost, Paktia, and Paktika.

[3] Constantinople Conference – held 23 Dec 1876 to 20 Jan 1877 in Constantinople (Istanbul) when the 'Great Powers' - Britain, Russia, France, Germany, Austria-Hungary and Italy attempted to settle nationalistic territorial differences in the Balkans that eventually evolved into the 1877-78 Russo-Turkish War.

someday – most likely when Russia finds herself a little more ready for war than she is at the present moment.

That is an amusing account of Lord Maidstone's marriage[1] – what a silly affair on both sides. I have a young gentleman who has just gone & done the same thing. His father is of an old Kent family Lushington & the boy[2] got engaged to a young lady at home before he came out here. His father would not hear of it & partly I believe to get the boy out of the way, sent him out to this country. A short time ago he heard stories that he had acted badly to the girl & like a young fool wrote & asked her to let it be on again, which she replied to by telegram saying the ship in which she was coming out & no time to stop her. The father does not agree to the son's marriage, but I add, being of age must please himself. The young lady is just 18 – the son is one of 10 children & the mother of the young lady ekes out her income by taking in children whose parents are in India & want a home for their children. So I should imagine their future career does not promise brightly.

They were married in Bombay some 3 weeks back & return here next week. They say the young lady has £100 a year of her own & what his father may give him – which under the circumstances I fancy will not be much.

It certainly is not a large sum that Russell offers Dick – hardly worth his taking, without a prospect of doing better in the future – I should imagine young Way[3] thought he would make something out of the farm & object to anyone being put in – of course anything that you

---

[1] George William Heneage Finch-Hatton, Viscount Maidstone (1852-1879), eldest son of Earl of Winchilsea married Louisa Augusta Jenkinson, daughter of Sir George Jenkinson 11th Bt. on 28 Dec. 1876.
[2] Lt. Edward Charles M Lushington (33rd Regiment) and Mary Hume were married by the Garrison Chaplain in Bombay on 31st January 1877.
[3] John Lewis Way of Spaynes Hall, Essex – cousin of Mrs Augusta Russell.

like to send Dick in the box for me I shall be very glad to contribute & Minnie will pay you the amount if you ask her – whatever it may be.

It is very kind of you being troubled with some of the children at Easter as you so kindly propose. No doubt the chicks will be charmed at the idea and their sightseeing in London. I will not say anything about Minnie & the children as no doubt she keeps you up in all their doings. Mr Gosselin seems wonderfully well & able to do a good deal but Mrs G still confined to the house with her leg. Lizzy seems all right.

I hope Robert Carey's son has qualified. It will be a great disappointment to his father if he does not. What a number of competitors went up – no wonder that nothing is done for officers when the supply is so much greater than the demand. I hope none of my boys will think of the army, it is the worst trade out nowadays.

No chance now of Charlie Denison or anyone else getting to Constantinople – India at the end of the year will probably be their destination, if nothing interferes in the interim.

Ned seems to find it hard to get anything to do.

Sorry to hear Helen has been suffering from Neuralgia[1].

The new doctor Col. Smith Dorrien called in seems to have done him good – insists no doubt on his orders & prescriptions being carried out…

---

[1] Neuralgia is a severe pain often described as stabbing or burning – resulting from a damaged nerve in any part of the body. It often occurs in the face or neck and its causes are many, from diabetes, an infection, shingles and others - the treatment depends on the cause.

Am glad you like the bit of onyx that May sent you – [Gerry] picked up a stone & had it polished & set as a pin for me from the same place & it makes a very pretty pin. I got it a short time ago when Capt. Fawcett came out.

Next week, I expect to hear of Major Johnstone['s] arrival in Bombay, he got his Regt'l majority by poor Weeding's death last year & will no doubt command the Reg't soon, as Chadwick only waits to be gazetted before he sends his papers in to retire. The same as I have done now, and he told me the other day, he regretted I had done so as he would have liked to have got home in my place. Of course, it makes a great difference to him retiring as a major or colonel – nearly £80 a year.

Do not write any more letters out to me here for I shall if all goes well, have left. How glad I shall be to see you all again. I am afraid this is a stupid epistle enough but there is little to make a letter lively from this.

I hear[d] from Frank Tupper today, giving me an account of his wanderings which he seems to have enjoyed.

With best love to all at Halkin Street & Wilton Place & same to self – ever dearest Mother

Your most affectionate son

Basil

Do not tell Minnie that I was so bad with liver. I have only said I had been feeling very sick. Mustard poultices[1] were no use & painting

---

[1] Mustard poultices - a mustard plaster made of mustard seed powder spread on a dressing and applied to the site of the pain to stimulate healing and helping to warm muscle tissues and chronic aches and pains.

my side with iodine[1] the only thing that did me good & relieved me. I am still taking stuff from the Doctor but have left off painting the iodine.

---

[1] Painting iodine onto the body allowed adsorption to compensate for deficiency of natural iodine in the system.

Letter from Thomas Basil Fanshawe to his mother

H M S 'Jumna'

Monday March 26th (1877)

My Dearest Mother,

I was so busy with one thing and another before I left Bombay that I had not time to send you a line & I know Minnie would keep you informed about my movements.

I had a deal of difficulty about getting a free passage home but at the last moment had the good luck to get a telegram to say it was granted & though I should have come home in this ship, as Capt. D'Arcy[1] would have given me a passage - still it is pleasanter not being indebted to anyone particularly when one has a right to a passage – as I am!

We left Bombay on Tuesday the 13th & shall have been out a fortnight tomorrow & so far have had a prosperous voyage. Though rather hotter some days, now quite pleasant. We did not stop at Aden[2] or anywhere & are now close to the Gulf of Suez – & Suez itself we expect to reach early on Wednesday morning, go part of the way thro' the canal that day – out of it the next & on our way to Malta, which we hope to reach on the 3rd April.

I shall see Selina there if still on the island & then a clear run to England which I shall be delighted to see again in good time.

---

[1] Captain John D'Arcy - commanded HMS Jumna from 4 October 1875 to 17 October 1877.

[2] Aden is situated on the eastern approach to the Red Sea with a natural harbour that lies in the crater of a dormant volcano, now part of a peninsula joined to the mainland by a low isthmus. Aden approximately equal distance from the Suez Canal, Bombay, and Zanzibar was vital to those important British possessions during the nineteenth century, when it was administered as part of British India.

I have been pretty well since I came on board & Capt. D'Arcy says I look better than when I came out with the Reg't. But I do not get quite right & must trust to cooler climes getting me right. I am quite sure that I have done wisely in retiring as I do not think I would have stood another Kamptee hot season & every one of my old friends say I have done the best thing.

We have the 11th Reg't[1] on board, a very nice quiet lot & they do not seem much excited at the idea of quitting that gross sham – India. I suppose their long residence there has made them feel rather washed out. All I know is, I would not go back to be made Governor General, not that there is much chance of that – but I declare I would sooner break stones in England than go back. I feel so low & depressed, the effects of the climate.

After leaving Malta we shall be at Plymouth if all goes right, about the 14th April. Plymouth is not usually called at but the 11th are to be quartered there – so I shall land there & get up to Bath in some 6 or 7 hours by train[2].

I wrote in one of my last for Minnie to meet me at Portsmouth if she could manage it as if she arrived late on 15th, Sunday is the 16th & as it is a cross line to reach Bath, I might have had to kick my heels about till Monday. Of course, I shall be only too charmed I she does come to Plymouth - but as it would only make the difference of 6 or 7 hours in meeting, it would save her the trouble & journey down.

---

[1] The 11th Regiment spent most of the nineteenth century on garrison duty throughout the Empire and in 1873 it received the depot at Topsham Barracks in Exeter. Under the Childers Reforms of 1881 the regiment became The Devonshire Regiment.

[2] By 1877 the railway network was sufficiently well establish to allow TBF to make connections through to Bath by leaving Plymouth on the Great Western Railway and connecting onto the Midlands Railway line.

I can hardly realise that in another 14 or 20 days I shall be with you all again!

I am wondering if you have had the children up to town? It is very kind of you being troubled with them & no doubt they will have been delighted with their visit. I shall be glad to hear what you think of them, if they did go – I shall doubtless find them much grown & I hope obedient…

Minnie was wonderfully pleased at the idea of my coming home. I am afraid she has fretted a good deal at my absence but now I hope she will see things in a brighter light. Please do not say more than - I am not quite right yet. I only wish it was the 15th of April instead of the 26th March.

I have had no letters since I left Kamptee but hope to find some either at Port Said or Suez & Malta. We get thro' the time on board by reading & playing whist[1] at which latter amusement I have been, so far, a winner – a most unusual thing for me as I hold as a rule very bad cards.

I have Doctor Fuller[2] in the cabin with me & had my passage been granted earlier, I should have had a cabin to myself. But we get on very well together & find we have plenty of room – much more than the Reg't had when we came out. Though the ladies that are on board complain that they & their children are crowded.

I will leave this intensely stupid production open till tomorrow, but I thought you would like a line however short.

---

[1] Card game requiring tactics and strategy that has origins in the sixteenth century - first played on scientific principles in 1728 by the gentlemen who frequented the Crown Coffee House in Bedford Row, London.

[2] Surgeon Major Samuel Fuller MRCS, LSAL (1833 – 1898) retired in 1886 as Honorary Surgeon General.

I was very seedy just before leaving Kamptee but I attribute that to the worry & bother of leaving the old Reg't.

I had to undergo the infliction of a farewell dinner which I would gladly have escaped had it been possible & my health was proposed & drank in a most complementary manner and I do not think a single officer was absent! It was rather a trial leaving a Reg't in which one had spent so many long & happy years, but it was only anticipating the time by a few months.

Chadwick intended going away to Simla for 4 months, so Johnstone would command – Chadwick will, I believe retire as soon as he is gazetted to the command.

Conor my old adjutant is on board with his child which is pleasant for both of us.

Tuesday, evg. – 27th March

We shall be in Suez early tomorrow morning & I hope half way thro' the Canal this time tomorrow night. We have had a strong head wind all day which makes us feel the difference of the temperature & what we may expect on the other side of Port Said. Luckily, I have the warm clothing I brought out with the Reg't, so I hope I shall not find the change so much.

I must close this stupid production – so with best love, ever dearest Mother.

Your most affectionate son

Basil

The

Retirement

Years

1877 – 1905

Queens Square, Bath
By Unknown – G. N. Wright (1864)
The Historic Guide to Bath – R.E.Peach
Public Domain

Once Basil Fanshawe had made the decision to retire, he put aside his long military career and launched himself into civilian life. With the uncertainty of his financial future resolved, he seems not to look back as he began to anticipate making the rest of his life happy and purposeful.

When HMS 'Jumna' docked at Plymouth, all remaining apprehension seems forgotten as he eagerly boarded the fastest train home to Emily and the children. Aware that without the routine and structure of the Army he would need to make changes. After dedicating all his time and energy into re-establishing his family life, it was obviously his resolve to then seek out recreational distractions to provide him with purpose and social entertaining companions through shared interests.

Close to his mother as a child, Basil had learnt it was important to make sensible use of time; a lesson taught as she schooled him into the self-discipline required for a successful army career. Mrs Fanshawe came from a military family and her father, Guernsey born Major General John Gaspard Le Marchant, had constantly impressed upon all his children the need to not waste any moment. He encouraged them to practice their individual talents but insisted their wide education should include foreign languages. He planned that with their 'accomplishments' they could confidently enter good society.

The Major General had met a hero's untimely death in 1812 at the head of the Heavy Brigade charge against the French army at the Battle of Salamanca in the Peninsula War. His act of courage was so celebrated[1] it almost came to overshadow his previous illustrious

---

[1] Watched by Wellington, who immediately afterward, declared *'I never saw anything more splendid in my life'* (foreword: David G Chandler -1997). – Re-published: Memoirs of the Late Major General Le Marchant – Denis Le Marchant (1841).

military record whereby having sought and obtained royal patronage, he set up and established the first Royal Military College at Marlow. From this beginning evolved the Royal Military College, Sandhurst where today Le Marchant is still recognised as a beacon of advanced thinking. He redesigned the standard army sabre and initiated and devised a training programme for the education of officers. Through his vision of disciplined officer training, he set the British Army on course to enjoy the reputation it holds today.

The strength of Le Marchant's personality remained an indelible force throughout the lives of his children and grandchildren. His high achievement with a spirit of service and duty continued to influence the family for many generations.

Schooldays

As parents, Mrs Fanshawe and the Rev. Thomas Lewis Fanshawe recognising that each of their children had different personalities and destinies they wisely planned their education accordingly. Their eldest son John Gaspard was expected to inherit the family seat of Parsloes Manor, and as was the way with past first born sons of the family, he anticipated a life as a country gentleman. Similar to his own father, he was educated at Eton College. Perhaps this became an advantage to him when expectations of society changed, for in his time it became fashionable and necessary for a serious gentleman to have a paid occupation. No doubt his school and family connections led him to take up his career in the offices of Parliament.

Inwardly, Mrs Fanshawe might have been thinking to encourage her eldest son towards an army career. It is possible that she gifted him a tactical game called the Game of Besieging. John was clearly the owner as he wrote his name on the box, but surely it was a game that Basil would have enjoyed playing...

Major General John Gaspard le Marchant
Henry James Haley
Defence Academy of the United Kingdom
Public Domain

The Game of Besieging Inscribed in ink on the case 'belonged to John Gaspard Fanshawe 1839'

Basil was not sent to Eton but stayed nearer to home for longer. Perhaps he was waiting for his younger brother Richard to reach the age when he could board with him for they both travelled to Shrewsbury School at the start of the autumn term of 1844. Basil was fifteen years old and we know a little of their activities from letters[1] written by their sister Helen Denison (née Fanshawe).

Eighteen year old Helen had married during the month of May that year. Her wedding was at her father's church of St. Peter and St. Paul, Dagenham[2] and soon after she left with her new husband Edward Hansen Denison[3] to take an extended European tour. The couple did not return until early the next year, after following an itinerary that took in many cities. From their hotel lodgings they despatched frequent letters home. A letter from Frankfurt in June 1844 reveals how at Dagenham Vicarage there were preparations in hand for the two boys to start their new school in the autumn term: *'I quite forgot Basil & Richard will be at home – pray give them my love and tell them I hope their first half year at Shrewsbury will prove a very happy one.'*[4]

Later that summer, the Rev. Fanshawe took his wife and two younger sons to the small town of Seaview on the Isle of Wight. During that holiday Basil began to learn to swim: *'I am surprised to hear Basil has taken such a fancy to the sea. I should rather thought it was much to Richard's taste…I hope they will like Shrewsbury, I have no doubt they will be happy when they are once settled'.*[5]

---

[1] Valence House, Archives & Local Studies Centre - original unpublished letters (1844/5) from Helen Denison to her mother and others of the Fanshawe family at Dagenham Vicarage.

[2] Parish church of Dagenham Village – mainly 15th Century.

[3] Edward Hanson Denison, (born 1814) Rusholme Park, Manchester.

[4] Letter from Edward Hansen Denison (Frankfurt) - June 1844.

[5] Letter from Helen Denison (Geneva) - August 1844.

The boys settled very well and apparently entered into the social activities of the school with enthusiasm: *'Give Basil and little <u>chimney sweeper</u> Dick my very best love and say I am delighted to hear the masquerade ball at Shrewsbury went off so well – I long to see them again and hear how they have enjoyed their first half year at a public school'.* [1]

The Duke of Wellington's 33rd Regiment

There are no further reports from Shrewsbury but when Basil finished his education he must have already decided upon his chosen career for he enlisted on 14th April 1846 as an Ensign with the 33rd Regiment of Foot[2]. The Regiment has not retained a record of his first posting but from their records confirm that between 1843 and April 1848 the 33rd was stationed at Halifax in Nova Scotia.

In letters written from Crimea in 1856, Basil indicated his familiarity with aspects of living in 'America', leaving us to assume he spent time in North America: *'on Saturday when shooting, all the frogs were chirping in chorus, which in America is a sure sign of approaching warm weather'*[3] and *'about as cold a day as I ever had the pleasure of being out in, even in America'.*[4]

The 33rd Regiment arrived back in the United Kingdom in the late spring of 1848 and passed a few months in Edinburgh, then Manchester before moving on to Berwick upon Tweed, Newcastle, Edinburgh and Glasgow.

On 15th November 1852 the Regiment was brought to London in preparation for the state funeral of the Duke of Wellington that took

---

[1] Letter from Helen Denison (Paris) - 24th December 1844.

[2] The name of the Duke of Wellington was not added to the regiment's title until his death in 1852. The 'Iron Duke's' original regiment had been the 33rd and therefore received his name in commemoration.

[3] Letter April 7th 1856 – *Sebastopol to Dagenham* (2016) Valence House Publications.

[4] Letter February 22nd 1856 – *Sebastopol to Dagenham* (2016).

place three days later. The 33[rd,] as the original regiment of the 'Iron Duke', were given a special invitation to participate. Very possibly Lt. Basil Fanshawe[1] took part in that splendid procession.

The records then show that for a few months the 33rd spent time in Manchester before being transferred to Ireland where the soldiers remained until 1854, when they embarked for war in Crimea.

Marriage

Bringing together these facts we create a picture reflecting career experiences that may have applied to many officers in Basil's time. These soldiers were active men but because of service far from home many found their opportunities for building personal relationships leading to courtship and marriage were limited. For serving men marriage was often impossible and many only began to contemplate or even afford family life once they had retired.

Basil Fanshawe was more fortunate, marrying at the age of thirty-five in 1864. Perhaps his opportunity came with the prospect of purchasing his commission and promotion to the rank of Major[2]. Although we cannot confirm if he and Emily were introduced by family connections, it is highly probable. The Bath Chronicle dated 16th April 1863 tells us he attended the Bachelors' Ball held at the Assembly Rooms the previous Thursday and from the same source, we know Emily Gosselin was also at the Ball. Their engagement was formally announced in the press on 7th January 1864.

We have only Basil's words and actions from which to make this opinion, but it seems he was a caring family man and a loving father. Although often constrained by distance, all indications are

---

[1] Harts Army List – 33rd Regiment 1852.
[2] For details of the loan he incurred with his brother John Gaspard - see private notes to Catherine Fanshawe – India letters.

that he tried to support his wife as she encouraged and educated their children in his absence. Once he had retired, it seems clear that he was very involved and spent time influencing his children to cultivate interests and pursuits as he attempted to expand their horizons.

Retirement to the City of Bath

In retirement Basil had no need to further record his life through letters and there is nothing more from him that documents his remaining thirty years.

Fortunately there are reliable sources to be found and a particularly fulsome obituary printed at his death in the Bath Chronicle & Weekly Gazette (7th May 1905) has been invaluable. With that as our guide, and contemporary archived newspapers we have traced an outline of his life after the army.

In all his actions and in whatever company he kept, Basil revealed that he was by nature a team player. Remaining true to his type, he took up a wide variety of activities and then, because he wanted his interests to thrive, he offered all the talents he had to those favoured organisations. Consequently, wherever he gave support, invariably he took on official responsibilities, leaving his name to stand out in those records.

He had many talents but perhaps most admirable was his dependable ability to stay the course. His innate reliability never allowed for short term interest and in his obituary, it is notable that all the many societies and clubs with which he was associated refer to his long and active membership. Loyalty and commitment were the binding threads to his life - long service to his regiment, family, marriage and faithful correspondence with his mother.

Park Street, Bath
Basil Fanshawe's home was on the right
(after the scaffold)
Derek Alexander (2018)

No 28

Derek Alexander (2018)

Settling in

Arriving home from India at the end of March 1877, Basil must obviously have found his six children growing up fast and it would have soon become clear that 28 Park Street[1] was too small to accommodate Emily and her children, her parents and unmarried older sister Elizabeth (Lizzie). Elderly parents, six children and two masters in one household, was hardly an ideal arrangement but it was soon resolved when Basil and his family moved to nearby 20 Park Street[2] then later to 24 Park Street[3].

With his domestic arrangements settled, Basil must have been ready to enjoy his first English summer for many years. Unfortunately, the summer of 1877 was particularly wet but unless rain stopped play, little would have deterred him from watching Lansdown Cricket Club in nearby Coombe Park.

He was to become one of the club's most regular supporters and with his gift for conversation it could not have been long before he was drawn into the easy banter enjoyed by sportsmen everywhere. Eventually he became one of the club's two Vice-Presidents and surely was proud of his association with one of the oldest and premier cricket clubs in the country. No doubt a regular source of conversation around that cricket field was the club's history with the legendary W. G. Grace, as he had played for Lansdown during the 1850's, when two other sons of the Grace family were club members.

---

[1] 1871 Census - 28 Park Street occupied by Mr & Mrs Gosselin, it passed to their single daughter Lizzie and later to Basil's son Herbert Cecil Fanshawe who resided there until his death in 1952.
[2] 1881 Census.
[3] 1891 Census.

The Sportsman

In common with most all-round sportsmen, Basil encouraged his children to take up many sports and the timing of his retirement was perfect to get them started. His two elder sons, Gerard eleven years old and Bertie a year younger, were being educated at Bath's Hermitage School, a short walk from their home. As they were 'day boys' their father had the opportunity to plan their recreation time.

Team sports were just starting to be formally established and physical activities were becoming acknowledged as vital for the health and well-being of young people. It was viewed that by promoting an 'esprit de corps' and loyalty on the field, responsible behaviour would follow.

Public schools had begun to form competing teams and sport was fast becoming accepted as an important part of education. These ideas were not new to Basil; this team building approach was consistent with modern military practices. The Army taught that a company of all abilities led to collective achievement when respect was shared.

Already, Basil had thought of directing his sons to military careers and he knew colleges were training young officers in these disciplines: [1] *'I should rather like to see a prospectus of the college near Oxford for sons of officers that you mention, it sounds well'.*

Modern officers in the Victorian army were receiving the specialised officer training as conceived by Basil's grandfather. They understood better that armed combat could only function if strengths and weaknesses were shared, and when forceful personalities together with the more modest knew their collective value. Old strategies and tactics must adapt to the conflicts in the

---

[1] May 26th 1876 – TBF to Mrs Catherine Fanshawe.

new colonies of India and Africa, so vastly different to those of old Europe.

Understanding these ideas places Basil ahead of his time - later this philosophy formed the basis upon which the Boys Brigade, Scouts and Church Lads Brigades emerged to be so popular in the early twentieth century. Those organisations were never intended for mere pleasure but were to promote the ethos of 'a good citizen' improving society who would be ready to serve.

Basil's enthusiasm for cricket, rugby football and almost every sport comes through in his letters. His social personality was at its most comfortable when he took part, but in common with most sportsmen, he enjoyed not only the exhilaration of the game but also the celebration and camaraderie surrounding the events.

It is no surprise that each of Basil's sons followed his example and as they strived to be good amateur sportsmen they made friends through those interests. Bath's local newspapers regularly reported sports days, galas, tournaments and other sports gatherings where the name Fanshawe was consistently included at all levels. As young schoolboys, they were reported as only in 'the heats' but later they became 'winners'. Even an egg and spoon race had to be taken seriously…

Less frequently, but also mentioned in newspaper sports columns were the Fanshawe girls – perhaps their mother Emily encouraged them too, for in her 'teens she had been a champion archer.

Besides Lansdown Cricket Club, the boys played for Bath F.C. which had been founded by earlier Lansdown players as a winter outlet for their energy during the cricket off season. Basil helped to run that club too, serving for many years as the senior Vice-President. Encouraged by their father, the Fanshawe boys played regularly in the teams with sports reports describing them in 'useful' terms.

With so many young men in those clubs, it is easy to imagine a busy social scene attached and most possibly Basil's third son, Reginald (Reggy) found his wife in those circles. Susan MacTier was the daughter of Robert Ferguson MacTier who was another Vice-President of Bath F. C. Her brother John, played for Somerset County but also played alongside Reggy as a three-quarter back in the Bath 'A' team.

Basil Fanshawe never exhausted his enthusiasm for sport, although it came as a surprise to discover that he helped to introduce the game of badminton to the townspeople of Bath. In India he had not consider the game of any interest '*there is very little doing in the station just now, only one Badminton night in the week at the Artillery mess – but I do not care for this & stick to my racquets*'[1]. Obviously he came to see that the game had merit for according to newspapers in both 1884 and 1885, his name was first on the list for the committee being formed to arrange tournaments. As he was not listed as a competitor, we must assume his pleasure was in organising the event.

Strangely, there is no evidence of activity for Basil's favourite game of racquets, although before his time in Bath the town had been one of the first to have a court.

The Gentlemen's Club

Before Basil found all those sporting activities, one of his early priorities on retirement must have been to arrange his membership at a gentlemen's club. In the first weeks after arriving home, domestic life must have been very hectic at Park Street compared to the peace and quiet in the spacious bungalow at Kamptee. Adapting

---

[1] Letter from Kamptee - April 8th 1876.

The Bath and County Club in 21-22 Queen Square
decorated for the marriage of Prince George,
Duke of York and Princess Mary of Teck in July 1893
The Bath Magazine website

The Royal Mineral Water Hospital, Bath (1943)

Frances Macdonald (1914 - 2002)

and sharing a house with six attention-demanding children aged between three and twelve years old, needs considerable patience.

The Bath & County Club was a haven of peace where a gentleman could escape the domestic scene - the membership was exclusively male and by election only and it occupied one of the beautiful town houses in Queen's Square, built by the architect John Wood the elder.

At his club, Basil could pass his time reading, playing billiards, bridge or even skittles, whilst discrete staff dressed in the club's livery of Oxford grey coat and trousers, with a scarlet waistcoat resplendent with club buttons, would attend to his needs. There were rooms for smoking and a library, and if he wished for company, there was a bar where he might find other local gentleman - many from the military. In that comfortable atmosphere, conversation must have been pleasurably reminiscent of a regimental mess - an environment always convivial for Basil.

If we judge from his obituary, it was a place where as a retired Colonel he was happy - where he could retain the same air of bonhomie we first got to know through his letters as a young captain in Crimea.

Community & Society

Although the Pump Room has always been one of the most important social and public places in the beautiful city of Bath, access was allowed by law to the poor, from the 16th century. All could make use of the healing waters of the Roman Baths and the famous health-giving thermal mineral waters, and from that charitable concept a hospital was promoted and founded in 1738 by Beau Nash and other socialites. By Basil's time it had become the

Royal Mineral Water Hospital and enlarged and expanded it offered healing treatments for rheumatic diseases.[1]

The hospital, locally known as the 'Min' became another of the causes that Basil Fanshawe found worthwhile to support. Volunteering his time and interest, he became a Governor of the hospital and for many years was the Chairman of the House Committee. By helping unfortunate people gain access to specialist treatment he possibly experienced a degree of personal satisfaction, for he had found an effective way of using his valuable professional organisational skills.

Another different facet of Basil's community approach to life came to light through learning of his latent interest in politics. Fanshawe family members had normally been reluctant to take part in political life, despite early ancestors with official appointments close to the seat of power. Normally in establishment posts they found it prudent not to adopt a public political view.

Such a cautious attitude had come down from Thomas Fanshawe (1534 – 1603), Queen Elizabeth's Remembrancer of the Exchequer, a courtier closely allied to the Queen's First Minister Lord Burghley. In the Remembrancer's role he had remained apolitical and after him those of the family following him into that office, generally maintained a similar profile. The notable period of exception being support of the Royalist cause during the Civil War.

Basil Fanshawe no doubt considered that by 1885 he could break that tradition when he enthusiastically became a founder member of

---

[1] The hospital is now incorporated into the local NHS Trust.

the Bath Habitation of the Primrose League[1]. The league was co-founded by Randolph Churchill and aimed to support God, Queen, country and the Conservative cause. It was intended to effectively represent the interests of members so that the experience of the leaders could be shared for the common good. Aspiring to improve the leader's professionalism and fight for free enterprise, membership was invited across the classes and all were encouraged to attend programmes of social activities with opportunities to meet Conservative politicians.

The Western Daily Press of 21st April 1885 reported the inaugural meeting held in the Assembly Rooms at Bath. The Duke of Beaufort presided as Ruling Councillor of the Habitation and two other gentlemen, one of whom was Basil Fanshawe, were elected to the Executive Council. Basil maintained his membership for many years, hosting and becoming acquainted with many of the leading Conservative politicians of the day.

Unfortunately, he is not included in a list of attendees at the Queen Victoria Jubilee event of the Habitation on 26th July 1897 which took place at Claverton Manor near Bath. It was an event that Basil would have greatly enjoyed - a summer event on the downs with races - perhaps ill-health kept Basil away?

Those fortunate to be there heard Winston Spencer Churchill, Randolph Churchill's twenty-three year old son, deliver his first political speech. He spoke against Home Rule in Ireland, pushed for compensation for injured workman and extolled his belief in liberal politics. The speech was reported by the newspapers as 'brilliant' and it was so well received the report was printed across the country[2].

---

[1] Named for Benjamin Disraeli the Tory Prime Minister who when he died in 1881 was sent a wreath of primroses with the inscription "His favourite flowers: from Osborne: a tribute of affectionate regard from Queen Victoria".
[2] The Bath Chronicle, 27th July 1897.

At Home

With his many varied activities, Basil Fanshawe must have been quite well known in Bath during his time and his involvement on so many committees tells us much about his character and the efforts he made to be useful in his community. Yet through his public life we gain only one dimension to his personality.

Whilst Basil's diary may have been filled with times and dates for all his activities, when we read official reports of those events we find that his wife Emily is not mentioned. Possibly, she and Basil were together at many of those social gatherings, but when other wives have been mentioned, we have not found Emily's name.

As a middle aged women, perhaps Emily was preoccupied giving loving support to her aging parents as presumably she could not leave her unmarried and older sister Elizabeth to care alone for Mr & Mrs Gosselin. Living nearby at 28 Park Street, both parents were fortunate to survive well into old age; Gerard Gosselin was ninety-three when he died in May 1888 and his Mrs Emily Gosselin, although eleven years younger and long suffering poor health, did not die until 1894, having reached the age of eighty-eight.

'Accomplishments' and Mrs Catherine Fanshawe

The other senior member of Basil's family was his mother, Catherine Fanshawe. We know from these India letters that she was active and healthy at the age of eighty and was still living in London at 15 Gloucester Street, Warwick Square.

After retirement it must have been pleasant for Basil to visit his mother in London, perhaps staying a night or two. Sadly those visits must have been too few, for Mrs Fanshawe died at the age of eighty-four on 6th July 1881 when she was staying with her daughter Helen Denison in Hertfordshire. She was buried alongside Helen's husband Edward Denison in Brompton Cemetery, London.

Without any doubt Mrs Catherine Fanshawe deserves special acknowledgement in any notes on Fanshawe family history but as the recipient and the original 'archivist' of Basil's letters, her personal story is of undeniable importance. Through her children's[1] letters she is revealed as an especially interesting lady, obviously in possession of a great strength of character and natural understanding.

From birth, her husband, Thomas Lewis Fanshawe could not have expected to inherit the family property of Parsloes for he was the fourth son of John Gascoyne Fanshawe. By all reports he was never in robust health, but he had the good fortune to have a wife with a maturity beyond her years. The Rev'd Thomas Lewis Fanshawe and Catherine Le Marchant proved to be a good match and the letters written by all her children are a testament to the love their mother brought to the Vicarage and Parsloes Manor. As her children reply to her regular letters they reveal such warm mutual understanding and it is clear that each one of them had their life underscored by her quiet energy as she 'silently' urged them to achieve what was possible.

Her eldest son John Gaspard Fanshawe was the first custodian of her letters after her death which included those sent by her own parents who died when she was young. The most poignant were written in 1811 and 1812 by her father, Major General John Gaspard Le Marchant – after his wife had died giving birth to their tenth child whilst he was serving in Spain with Wellington's army. Through eloquent, grammatical descriptions he mingled melancholy thoughts whilst revealing to his eldest daughter 'Katherine'[2] plans for her education. The letters tell of a different life she would have known had her father survived the war and returned to his position as Lt. Governor of the Royal Military College at High Wycombe and

---

[1] Collections of letters from Helen Denison (née Fanshawe) and Richard Fanshawe – Valence House Archives.

[2] Her father always addressed her as 'Katherine'.

Marlow. Katherine was to be his consort in society but sadly that was never to be and instead at fourteen, as elder sister of ten orphaned siblings, she quickly matured to give support to her younger brothers and sisters. This continued to be her role for the rest of her life.

Her father's expectations had been high and whilst his letters are beautiful and the descriptions vivid, they could be exceedingly blunt. He had no time to waste; never frivolous he explains his concern is only for her future: … '

do not take amiss what I have said – if I loved you less I should be more indifferent to whether you were well educated or not… It is alone the great affection that I bear you which makes me feel the most ardent desire that you shall be entitled to settle well in life which can be reasonably hoped for when the education has been carried to considerable perfection.

Beauty education & money are separately capable of obtaining an advantageous marriage – money I am sorry today is most sought after because the world is licentious.

Accomplishments have an undoubted preference to beauty because the latter without accomplishments is insipid & really no lasting impression on the sentiments of any but an idiot. As you have neither the money nor the beauty your whole reliance is on an excellent education.

I have said all this before but I am not mindful of the time & trouble that I take to render you my dear Katherine, everything that is perfect.[1]

As Major General Le Marchant died three weeks after this letter, it is difficult to imagine that his final words did not make an impact on his daughter's life. Catherine may have been less proficient at languages than he hoped and perhaps, as a harpist or pianist she

---

[1] Letter 5th July 1812 - John Gaspard Le Marchant (Nava de Rey, Spain).

never excelled – but her 'accomplishments' proved to be real and well beyond all his expectations. As a sophisticated officer he certainly would have been proud of her strength and dependability which gave confidence to her husband through her discrete quiet presence. Through her father's influence on her education and her own personality, she was perfectly suited to her dual role as the wife of a country vicar and the mistress of an historic country house.

Mrs Fanshawe experienced further tragedy two years after her father's death when her eldest brother Carey Le Marchant died from wounds also received whilst serving in Spain. Then only Catherine and her second brother Denis remained of sufficient age to keep alive their father's legacy.

Through all those dramatic events Denis Le Marchant shared his family grief and his room at Eton with his friend Thomas Lewis Fanshawe. Thomas Fanshawe then went on to St. Mary's Hall, Oxford whilst Denis Le Marchant continued his studies at Trinity College, Cambridge.

In 1821, four years after his induction as Vicar of Dagenham, Thomas Fanshawe married his friend's sister Catherine Le Marchant.

Denis Le Marchant took up a career in politics and became an M.P. and Under Secretary of State for the Home Department. From 1850 to 1871 he was Clerk of the House of Commons[1], which brought him a baronetcy. Denis, also a published historian, became his father's biographer[2] but he left military life to the younger Le Marchant brothers. Several made very successful careers but undoubtedly the highest ranking was John Gaspard Le Marchant the third son who

---

[1] The Clerk of the House is politically impartial and the principal constitutional adviser to the House.

[2] 'Memoirs of the late Major General Le Marchant 1766-1812 (Published 1841) – republished in 1997 by Spellmount Library of Military History.

was knighted and became Lieutenant Governor for Newfoundland & Nova Scotia, and Governor for Malta.

Many of the Le Marchant family were made welcome at the Vicarage in Dagenham and at Parsloes Manor in a period that lasted at least half a century. The names of some of the younger family members of Mrs Fanshawe may be found in the local parish registers, being married by the Revd. Fanshawe in his church at Dagenham village.

Travel between Guernsey and Dagenham was frequent. Britain had entered the age of great industrial and transport expansion and together with good regular mail services the ever-expanding families were in close touch. With access to sufficient financial means, they took advantage of modern facilities and stayed close; several inter-familial marriages resulted over several generations.

Through these letters we can see how strong affection and care was shared around the family. These comfortable relationships often show an individual's personality through their situation, so it is easy to feel real empathy with Mrs Fanshawe. Ironically we do not have one of her own letters written to her father or later, her children. Photographs and portraits of this special lady elude us - but perhaps within a family album there may lie her image waiting silently for our discovery. We hope that such a well-loved lady did not remain 'complexed' by her father's statement - making certain to avoid the artist's brush and the camera's lens.

Family

Basil Fanshawe, too occupied with his busy life to spend time with a private journal left us to seek other ways to view his private world. The first step to doing this is through the reports of formal social occasions that were often so graphically recorded in nineteenth century newspapers. Marriages and landmark celebrations were fully reported and we have located details of some Fanshawe activities in Bath, London and other parts of the country.

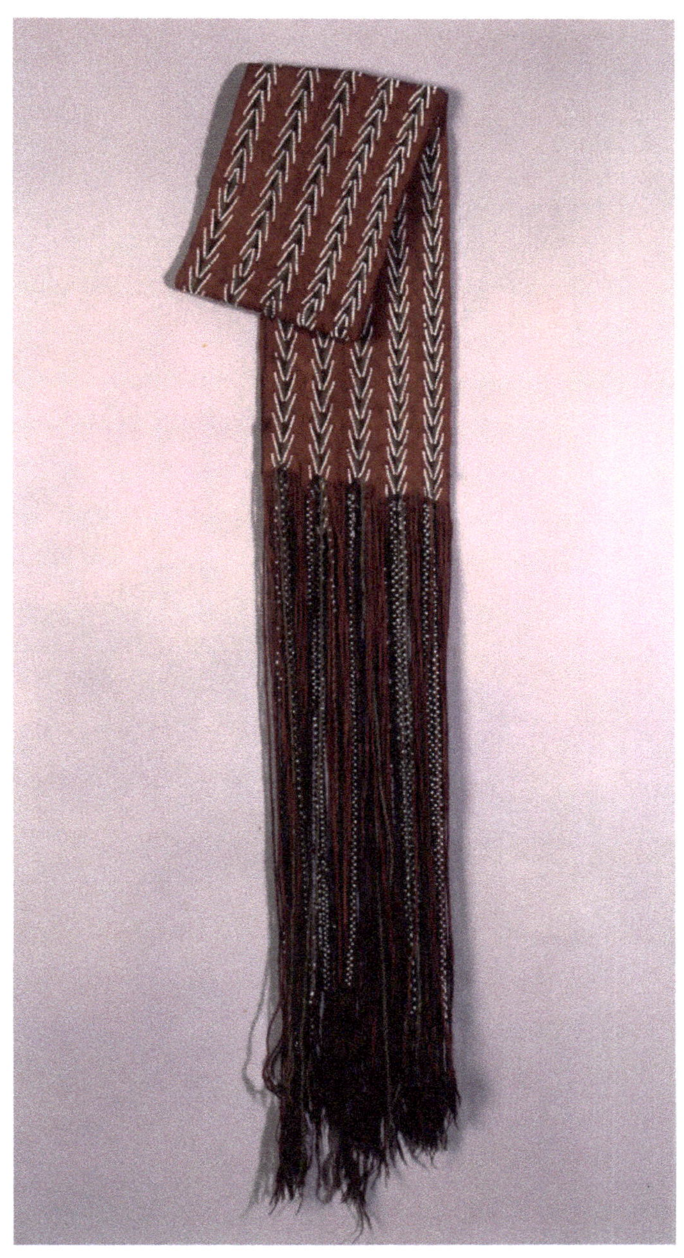

Belt - "Said by donor to be Maori and to
have been brought over from New Zealand
in 1860 by Richard Fanshawe for John G. Fanshawe."
British Museum

Companion of the Order of St Michael & St George
Awarded to Colonel Reginald Winnington Fanshawe
Chief Paymaster - New Years honours list 1917
Public Domain

We know that Mrs Fanshawe and her late husband tended to welcome their children's in-law relations into their own circle and from Basil's letters we learn that Emily and his mother were on good terms – carefully allowing each other respect. They would have been helped by having similar backgrounds, both families coming from the Channel Islands where they had many mutual relations.

Basil's letters show his particular relationship with his many aunts, uncles and cousins. Perhaps knowledge of their normal daily lives kept him grounded to reality when far from home. More understandable is his constant concern for his younger brother Richard – his childhood 'friend'. He obviously worries that the 'free spirit', reluctant to adopt a formal career, will eventually be left unfulfilled and is desperate that he has a prosperous future. 'Dick' always longed to travel and explore, even visited Basil at Sebastopol during the Crimean War and made the trip an adventure by travelling home via the tourist sights of the Middle East. As a young man, Dick's own letters are full of observations told with a great sense of fun, but later he has obviously been struggling to find purpose.

Basil writing from Abyssinia in 1868, reveals that Dick had tried several entrepreneurial schemes including surveying in New Zealand where he had lived since 1861. From Kamptee, after a decade, we hear from Basil that Dick still seeks an interesting occupation, and hopes to travel to 'The Cape'. We have found no evidence confirming he travelled to Africa, and know only that during 1878 he travelled from New Zealand to England on a visit to his family. When he returned to New Zealand he settle at Southbridge, Canterbury, where he died in 1902.

Basil's elder brother, John Gaspard was totally different – he made a career in parliament and became secretary to several cabinet ministers. He had a position at the Board of Trade which in view of the time period seems to imply that he was introduced into these offices by his uncle Denis Le Marchant. He inherited Parsloes Manor but finding it difficult to maintain, he eventually let the property and settled with his family in fashionable Belgravia. His wife Barbara Coventry, was a granddaughter of the 7th Earl of Coventry and together they had three sons and two daughters.

John Gaspard's eldest son Evelyn[1] was aged twenty-three when mentioned by Basil in the letters as 'Evy' – he was frustrated at the lack of direction in his nephew, despite having been educated at Eton. He warns that his brother John should be more firm with him: *'it is a pity he does not insist on Evy's doing something, anything better than idling about doing nothing at his age – a clerkship would be better than nothing. Evy would not like it perhaps? Basy[2] will do well when once started[3]...* Unfortunately, Basil was probably right as Evelyn continued to have trouble settling into a career, although records actually show that when Basil wrote Evelyn had enlisted in the West Essex Militia (1875) but he resigned his commission as Captain in 1887.

Basil was obviously by that time a good judge of character in young men, as John Gaspard's second son Basil did very well. Educated at Repton School, he displayed all the industry of his namesake, including an ability to focus. He was a good sportsman and played football for his school – obviously a team player that Basil would admire. When he left school he took up a modern civil engineering apprenticeship and then after three years changed tack and sailed to Ceylon[4] to become a tea planter. With his estates named Dagenham and Parsloes he became one of the first to start to produce rubber.

By 1891 his adventure had proved so successful that he had the means to retire back to England at the early age of thirty-six. He

---

[1] Evelyn - a family Christian name since the 17th century, it had been the family surname of Sarah, 2nd wife of the 2nd Viscount Fanshawe of Dromore (a cousin was John Evelyn, the diarist).

[2] Basil - probably TBF's godson.

[3] Letter from Kamptee – August 15th 1876.

[4] Sri Lanka.

bought an estate in North Devon and living in some style, expended a great deal of his time and energy tracking down and acquiring many of the family portraits and documents that had previously been sold by others in the family.

Basil died in 1944 when he was eighty-six but delightful descriptions of him and the other children of TBF's elder brother John Gaspard, have been vividly recorded by their nephew Strathearn Gordon. He tells his memories of the Fanshawe and Gordon families in his unpublished 'Storybook'. Although it was written during his own retirement in the 1980s, he recollects with clarity the aunts and uncles so familiar and loved in his youth. Through Strathearn's relatively modern eye, he presents a charming view of the early twentieth century experienced by a generation of the Victorian era, when codes of social behaviour were vastly different from today.

Memories of a very special aunt are recalled and tell of her lively character and personality - she was Basil's niece Beaujolois Mabel. Until now Mabel has perhaps been a little overlooked, but from India Basil mentions that John Gaspard's eighteen year old elder daughter has entered her debutante year[1]: *I should not have thought that John would have gone to the expense of sending Bab & Mabel to the drawing room this year'*. The euphemism implying presentation at Queen Victoria's court, confirms that 'Mabel' was launched into society in the season[2] of 1876 and even Basil makes comments on her attendance at the spectacular ball at Bisham Abbey[3] on the 21st December - widely reported in the press.

From the press we also find that Mabel with her mother Barbara Fanshawe (*Coventry*), then later with her husband Arthur Ridout, and her younger sister Violet were often guests at the best society weddings. Perhaps the most interesting and unusual was the

---

[1] Letter from Kamptee August 15th 1876.

[2] By tradition the annual period when it was customary for the social elite to hold balls, dinner parties and charity events.

[3] Letter from Kamptee January 20th 1877.

marriage[1] of a Coventry cousin to Prince Victor Duleep Singh, son of the last Maharaja of Lahore. The detailed description[2] of every guest and their gifts makes quite extraordinary reading today.

As Mabel matured she developed a passionate interest in the Fanshawe family history leading her to collaborate with a distant cousin H. C. Fanshawe researching and producing a written account of the family story. Until then the family history only existed in scattered papers and oral accounts handed down through generations but with their joint tenacity they brought the story to publication as 'The History of the Fanshawe Family'[3]; so relied upon today.

Anyone with an opportunity to explore 'The History' will soon realise that the way they structured, compiled and edited this extensive book was a major accomplishment. Without today's resources, the research was undertaken by both cousins travelling widely to track down original source material. An archive[4] now exists in Valence House that is full of papers, documents, notes and ephemera relating to the journeys and visits that they made taking in many libraries and country and stately homes. Assembling the vital facts, they produced a seminal work that has proven to be reliably correct and invaluable.

It would seem that H.C Fanshawe wrote the main body of the history but Mabel's contribution was considerable for her dynamic personal energy and endless 'field' work were essential after her cousin became seriously ill in 1921. He died two years later when the history was still incomplete and only Mabel's determination ensured that the family story was published in 1927.

---

[1] January 4th 1898.
[2] The Morning Post, London 5th January 1898.
[3] The History of the Fanshawe Family by H C Fanshawe - Andrew Reid & Co. Ltd (1927).
[4] The Fanshawe Collection (this archive at present uncatalogued).

The detailed pedigrees that lie between the five hundred pages are the work of Mabel and the extent of her difficulties in their preparation was witnessed by Strathearn Gordon – 'The Fanshawes in their separate branch pedigrees became so numerous that my Aunt set to work to combine them into one enormous pedigree[1], which first covered the table and then the entire floor, and had to be rolled. Thereafter, untold hours were spent kneeling and writing, with occasional pauses for a stroll and smoke in the garden at Codercum[2] or later in her London home in Philbeach Gardens'.

Within his 'Storybook', Strathearn's affectionate description of his especially engaging Aunt Mabel (thought of as a volcano) shows her ready wit and unpredictable temperament. He leaves an impression that she was one of the many Fanshawe ladies that must never be overlooked.

There have been many spirited ladies of the family who proved to be more than mere decorative ciphers to Fanshawe men. Most were fortunately aided by the enlightened views that their men had been handed down regarding marriage and equality in their daughters' lives. The will of Thomas Fanshawe (2nd Remembrancer) pointed the way towards security for their womenfolk - perhaps that founding common ancestor of the family left his influence to linger long?

Basil's sister Helen was another interesting lady of the nineteenth century family. We are only just beginning to learn more of her through her correspondence. Frequent letters were sent home from her European tour to the Vicarage and Helen reveals her maturity as a correspondent with assured impressions of art and society through affectionate letters addressed to her mother.

When the couple returned they had the means to live in comfort with their growing young family, but sadly Edward died in 1864. Helen had the financial security to live independently, immersing

---

[1] Deposited at Valence House, Archives & Local Studies Centre.
[2] Near to Newcastle upon Tyne – home of Beaujolois Mabel & Arthur Ridout.

herself firstly into the lives of her children and later indulged her passion for her large garden at her beautiful home in Hertfordshire. Basil's letters from India show his keen interest in his sister's welfare and particular concern for the careers of her three sons.

The elder son Edward Fanshawe Denison referred to as Ned, became a marine engineer and set up a company at Dartmouth. Obviously community spirited he took on the honorary role of secretary to the Royal Dart Yacht Club. His business was successful and he travelled widely: during a visit to Rome in 1898 he was suddenly taken ill and although he was able to return home, he died shortly after. He was only fifty years of age, and he and his widow Anna Dora née Cumberbatch, had no children.

Joseph Basil Denison (Joe) became a Colonel in the Leinster Regiment. He married Annie Louise Campbell in 1889 and had two children. Joseph died in 1917 at seventy-one, having spent his retirement in Kensington and with his sister at Little Gaddesden.

Albert Charles (Charlie), Helen's third son, lived at Bembridge, Isle of Wight - he did not marry and was only forty-four when he died in 1896.

The elder of all Helen's children was Helen, also mentioned by Basil from India when she was thirty years old. Four years previously she had married William Romilly whose father was Master of the Rolls. William, who had succeeded to his father's baronetcy in 1874, was a widower, having been married to Helen's cousin Emily Le Marchant, daughter of Sir John Gaspard Le Marchant. Basil's niece Helen had no children and died two years before her husband in 1889.

Basil's younger niece of the Denison family was Katherine. She never married and remained with her mother at Little Gaddesden where they received frequent family visitors to their lovely home. As can be seen from the census returns of 1901 and 1911 they enjoyed considerable comfort as nine servants were employed in the household. A team of gardeners who lived out, maintained their extensive gardens where medal-winning blooms were cultivated.

Outliving all her younger brothers, Helen Denison died at home in 1917 when she was ninety-one. When her daughter Katherine died in 1938 she joined her mother and father, brother Charlie, and her grandmother Mrs Catherine Fanshawe in the Denison family grave at Brompton Cemetery.

Basil's Family

Basil and Emily Fanshawe had no more children after he retired, their youngest child Frank, born in the Barracks at Fermoy in Ireland was just three years old but the time was soon coming for Basil to think seriously about the future careers of his elder sons.

Despite having said he would not recommend the Army to his sons: *'I hope none of my boys will think of the army, it is the worst trade out nowadays'.*[1] He must have later taken a more rational view and seeing the army was modernising, noted the new specialised units of service introduced which might offer a better life than in the traditional regiments of foot.

Basil's observation of Robert Napier's logistics in Abyssinia may have played some part, for in 1883 his eldest son Gerard Lewis Fanshawe (born 1866 in India) joined the Royal Engineers. Progressing well he was in a position to marry Grace Allenby in 1894 and her brother Edmund was his best man – later Field-Marshall Viscount Allenby G.C.B., G.C.M.G[2].

---

[1] Letter dated February 10th 1877.

[2] Veteran of the Boer War, Viscount Allenby (1861 – 1936) was engaged on the Western Front at the outbreak of World War I. In 1917, appointed by Prime Minister Lloyd George he took control of the Egyptian Expeditionary Force ('Lawrence of Arabia' came under his command) - his successful campaign lead to the recapture of the Middle East.

Gerard Fanshawe was promoted to Major by July 1902 but two years later whilst serving in Malta, he contracted and died of 'Maltese Fever'[1]. Sadly, he was only thirty-eight years old and he and his wife had no children.

Already in poor health, Basil was devastated by the loss of his eldest son. It is not too difficult to imagine what he might have said when he learned that Gerard had died in Malta for all his references to the island show a dislike as he found the dry relentless heat unbearable – *'am pleased Selina writes so favourably impressed with Malta – it is a place I never liked as a quarter'.*[2]

Basil's second son Herbert enlisted with the Submarine Miner Engineers[3] (Royal Engineers) in 1893. He retired fifteen years later with the rank of Honorary Major but he re-enlisted during the First World War and served in the Army Pay Department with his younger brother Reggy. He was fifty-four when finally he retired in 1919 and returned to 28 Park Street in Bath. After his mother died in 1926 at the age of 91, he continued living in the family home until he died unmarried in 1952.

One after another Basil's boys chose the military life. It was probably Reginald Fanshawe (Reggy) who became the career soldier, most similar to his father. He passed through the Royal Military College at Sandhurst and then at twenty joined the Duke of Wellington's 33rd Regiment.

Serving seven years with the 33rd, Reggy saw action in southern Africa then in 1898 he transferred to the Army Pay Department. The same year he married Susan MacTier from Bath and then saw action in the Boer War. By 1913 he had attained the post of Staff Paymaster

---

[1] The term used in Mediterranean counties for brucellosis, a bacterial illness normally caused by eating/drinking unpasteurized soft dairy products made from the milk of infected animals – often goats.
[2] Letter dated January 20th 1877.
[3] The defence of harbours through the use of submerged mines.

and during the First World War he was promoted to Colonel and Chief Paymaster and for that service he was awarded the C.M.G[1].

In 1899 his first child Nancy Peronelle was born and a sister Jean in 1914. Between those girls, a boy was born in 1908 and he was named Basil – three years too late for Basil Fanshawe to meet the only grandson who might continue his name.

Unfortunately, his name brought him no luck. He enlisted in the West Yorkshire Regiment in World War II, was promoted to the rank of major but was killed in action whilst serving in Burma during 1943. The last Basil Fanshawe is commemorated on the memorial in Rangoon - aged thirty-five, and unmarried.

Basil's youngest son, Frank took up fruit farming in Guernsey and in 1901 married Henrietta Carey, one of his distant Guernsey cousins[2]. They had two daughters, Joan and Faith.

Basil's elder daughter Helen Maude also married a cousin from Guernsey, Cecil Carey and over the next few years visits must have been frequent between Bath and Guernsey. Through these visits, probably came the next marriage between the two families - Basil's youngest daughter Lilian married Eugene Carey in 1910 – he was Helen's brother-in-law.

Lilian and Eugene Carey had no children but Helen and Cecil Carey had two daughters, Daphne and Eileen.

Through the daughters of Helen, Frank and Reginald Fanshawe, we may trace the descendants of Basil & Emily Fanshawe.

---

[1] Companion of the Order of St. Michael & St. George – services to the 'Empire'.
[2] Basil's mother Katherine Le Marchant was a daughter of Mary Carey.

***Virtutis Fortuna Comes**[1]*

After an illness of some weeks, Basil Fanshawe died at home on 4th May 1905 and his funeral followed days later with many people coming to mourn '*of a most genial nature, he was greatly liked by all with whom he was brought into contact* [2]... The representatives and friends were from the many organisations he had supported and encouraged over many years.

His wife Emily survived him and lived well beyond the First World War. She died at home during August 1926 at the great age of 91 ...'*it is surmised that she has been one of the oldest inhabitants of Bath*'[3].

Basil and his two brothers John Gaspard and Richard died in the space of a couple of years in that brief Edwardian period of the early 20th century. Their stories were too contemporary for detailed inclusion in 'The History of the Fanshawe Family' – they are almost of our time yet they remain distant. Basil's letters provide a pathway to take us back…his baton lies waiting, the Fanshawe story goes on.

…Then leaf subsides to leaf.
So Eden sank to grief,
So dawn goes down to day
Nothing gold can stay.[4]

---

[1] "Fortune is the companion of virtue"
Motto of Duke of Wellington's 33rd Regiment.
[2] Bath Chronicle & Weekly Gazette – 7th May 1905.
[3] The Bath Chronicle & Herald – Saturday August 7th 1926.
[4] *'Nothing Gold Can Stay' – Robert Frost (1874 – 1963)*

DEATH OF COLONEL FANSHAWE

A POPULAR BATH FIGURE

To the deep regret to a host of friends, Colonel T B Fanshawe passed away on Thursday evening at his residence in Park Street. He had been seriously ill for some weeks past, and it had been realised that any prospect of recovery was hopeless.

Colonel Fanshawe passed his military career in the 33rd Foot, now known as the West Riding Regiment, and served with that corps in the Crimea, where he took part in several actions. He landed in the Crimea in January 1855, and was present at the siege of Sebastopol and the assault on the Redan on the 18th June, receiving the medal and clasp and the Turkish medal. The 33rd were subsequently employed in India and the deceased officer was second in command of a wing of the regiment at the siege and capture of Dwarka, Okamendal in 1859. He served in the Abyssinian campaign of 1867-8 and was present at the storming and capture of Magdala for which he held the medal. He retired from the Army in 1878 with the rank of Honorary Colonel, and took up his residence in Bath.

Of a most genial nature, he was greatly liked by all with whom he was brought into contact and probably no member of the Bath and County Club will be more genuinely grieved for than this departed officer whose good humour and joking repartee made his presence always welcome. Many years ago he became a Governor of the Royal Mineral Water Hospital, and took a deep interest in the welfare of that institution. For a long while he had presided over the House Committee, a body on which the administration of the hospital chiefly devolves, and at the Annual Court the other day, reference was made by his colleague, the Rev. H. H. Winwood, to his regretted illness.

In politics Col. Fanshawe was a staunch Conservative and was one of the original knights of the Bath Habitation of the Primrose League when it was formed 29 odd years ago. For a considerable period he had had a seat upon the Council of the Habitation and in his capacity as Deputy Ruling Councillor frequently presided over Primrose gatherings at the Rooms.

The deceased gentleman was a thorough sportsman and attached to all manly games, in which he participated with much skill in his early days, while up to the last he was a regular and keen angler and a successful shot. The Lansdown Cricket Club loses one of its oldest friends and supporters by his death. He was one of the two Vice-Presidents of the Club, and seldom missed watching a match at Combe Park, and his cheery voice will be sadly missed from the spectators' enclosure. He was also the senior Vice-President of the Bath Football Club, and had been a constant attendant at its matches since the days when the team played in Kensington Meadows and some of his boys, who were educated at the Hermitage have been capable members of the Bath side.

Though not prominently associated with any local lodge, the deceased was a Freemason of long standing. The death of his eldest son Major Fanshawe, at Malta, last year, occasioned the gallant Colonel much grief, and it was noticed that he had never been really his old self since the sad news reached him. He leaves a widow and several sons and daughters.

THE FUNERAL

Amid many signs of great respect and affection in which he was held, the mortal remains of Colonel Fanshawe were interred at Locksbrook Cemetery on Monday. The funeral cortege left 24 park Street shortly before noon, the coffin bearing beautiful wreaths, while the floral tributes were so numerous that a special brougham conveyed them to the cemetery.

In the two mourning carriages were Capt. H. C. Fanshawe, Capt. R. W. Fanshawe and Mr F. R. Fanshawe (sons), Mrs G. Fanshawe (daughter-in-law), Mr C. A .Carey (son-in-law) and two nurses. The coffin was received at the chapel by the Rev. A. V. Gregoire, assistant priest of All Saints', Lansdown (the incumbent the Rev. W. H. Powell being prevented from officiating through absence from Bath), and the choir of the church. In the chapel, "Now the labourer's task is o'er" was sung, and at the graveside before the Benediction "On the Resurrection morning".

There was a large congregation of friends at the cemetery, including Mrs Cary, Miss Cary, Mr and Mrs R. F. McTier, Mr J. McTier, Captain Gostling and Miss Claxton. Representing the Royal Mineral Water Hospital were: Mr W. Kemble (president), Rev. H. H. Winwood (vice-president), Mr Robert C Bush (treasurer), Colonel M. P. Ricketts, Rev. G. F. Pearson and Mr J. E. Goddard Bradford (members of the committee), Dr Carter and Mr F. K. Green (hon medical and surgical staff), Rev T. Tyers (chaplain), Dr Waterhouse (resident medical officer) and Mr T. Kirby (registrar). Mr E. E. Phillips (Ruling Councillor), Major-General Coningham (hon. Secretary), and Capt. Ingham (hon. Treasurer) represented the Bath Habitation of the Primrose League.

Three old brother officers of the deceased in the 33rd (Duke of Wellington's) Regiment were present in the persons of Major-General W. Bally, Colonel C. Conor and Lieut.-Colonel R. H. Fawcett, while ex-Sergt. F. G. Woodward who served under the Colonel in the 33rd Regiment was also present.

Others present, among whom were many fellow members of the Bath and County Club included Admiral Sulivan, General Clement

Smith, General Maule, Mr M. H. Scott (brother churchwarden of the deceased at All Saints), Captain Huth, Mr M. St. John Maule, Mr A. K. Cuninghame, Captain Hardyman, Colonel Walker VC, General Sir John McQueen, Mr Claude Wade, General Blair, Mr R. S. Fowler, Mr J. T. Piper (representing the Bath Football Club), Dr Lionel Weatherby, Major Straghan, Mr Knight, Major Ormond, Mr Alfred Castellain, Colonel Little, R.E., Capt. Macintire, Mr May Somerville, the Rev. C. W. Shickie, Mr W. Morgan, Mr J. G. Le Marchant, Mr F Tupper, Mr Walter Brymer, the Rev. A. Pontifex, Prebendary Norton Thompson, Mr C. Y. Petgrave, Mr Langfield Ward, Mr Christopher Thring, Mr Stanley Wills, Mr Mercer Adam, Mr K. Macdonald, Mr H. F. Steward, Mr C. Gaine, Mr O. A. G. Collins, Surgeon-Major Scott, Colonel Wilkinson, Mr E. Elliott, Colonel Thomson, General Smith, Col. R. T. Gwyn, Mr R.G. H. Scott, Mr C. C. Gill, representing the SS Peter and Paul Chapter of Rose Croix: Mr J. Austin (National Provincial Bank) etc. Mr Henry Gore was prevented by indisposition from attending.

The interment was made in a new grave, which was lined with moss and edged with white roses, under the shade of a magnificent Chinese cherry, which was white with bloom. On the brass plate of the unpolished English oak coffin was the inscription "Thomas Basil Fanshawe, died May 4 1905, aged 75"

The wreaths and crosses came from:- Mrs Hobbs, Rev. C. W. Shickle, the three servants at 24 Park Street, the Miss Fanshawe (London), Mr Evey Fanshawe, Major Henry Maule, Mr Walter Maule and Miss Ethel Maule, Mr and Mrs St. John Maule, Mr and Mrs McTier, Mr J. McTier, Mrs Handley, Dr and Mrs Bannatyne, Mr and Mrs W. S. M. Goodenough, Mrs R. C. Price, Bath Primrose League (in memory of a dear friend and most useful colleague), the Bath Field Club, Lieut.- Col. R. H. Fawcett, Mr and Mrs W. Morgan, Mr and Mrs Rooke, Mr Robt. C. Bush, Mr and Mrs S. J. Sherer and Miss Dede Sherer, nurse and maids at 28 Park Street, Miss Gosselin, Mr and Mrs Neville Sturt, Mr Percy and Miss Phyllis Carey, Lewis Carey, Miss Dora Carey; Member of the Bath and County Club, the M.W.S. and Brethren SS Peter and Paul Red Croix, Mrs Tufnele, Major and Mrs Harry Gostling, Miss Selina Gostling and Miss Winifred Gostling, Admiral and Mrs Sulivan, the Misses Sulivan, Mr and Mrs Walter Brymer, General and Mrs Barlow, Mrs Goodwyn and the Misses Goodwyn, Miss Geraldine Serrell, Colonel and Mrs Seagram, Mr and Mrs Steward, Dr A. L. MacKenzie, the nurses, Mr Austin, Mrs Wilkieson, Col. and Mrs Northey, Capt. and Mrs Macintire, Mr Wiggett, Mr and Mrs Wade, Mr and Mrs Pakenham and Mrs Langdon, Capt. De Lancy Gostling, Misses Flo and Effie Brock, General and Mrs Blair and Miss Blair, Mrs Connolly and Miss Connolly, Miss Walker, Mrs Machell, Col. And Mrs Douglas and Miss Douglas, Mrs Henry Balguy, etc.

The funeral arrangements were carried out by Messrs Horton Brothers of Northgate Street.

REFERENCE AT ALL SAINTS'

The Rev. A. V. Gregoire M.A., assistant priest at All Saints', preaching on Sunday morning said : - Without detaining you for any length of time, I wish to say a few words this morning about the great loss that many people in this city, and more especially we who worship God in this church, have just sustained in the passing away to his eternal rest of Colonel Fanshawe. The life of such a man as he – an ideal English gentleman, respected and loved by all who knew him; a soldier who served his country with honour and what is most important of all, a faithful soldier and servant of Jesus Christ – the life of such a man as Thomas Basil Fanshawe is one of great gifts that God gives to us mortals, as an example for us to follow, and an incentive to spur us on to nobler and better things. And as we grow older, my brethren, it is one of the sad things in life to see these men of the old school – courteous gentlemen and sincere Christians – passing away from amongst us one after the other; and the highest honour we can pay to their memory is to see to it that there be others amongst us fit and worthy to step into the places that they vacate. I am quite sure that all of you, in your prayers to God today, will remember those who are now smarting under the pain of a great bereavement. –

At the morning service the organist (Mr. E.W. Cambridge) played the Dead March in "Saul" and in the evening Beethoven's "Funeral March for the death of a hero"

Bath Chronicle & Weekly Gazette – 7th May 1905

Grave of Colonel Thomas Basil Fanshawe
Locksbrook Cemetery, Bath
Derek Alexander (2018)

Grave inscription of Colonel Thomas Basil Fanshawe
Locksbrook Cemetery, Bath
Derek Alexander (2018)

Fanshawe family history – resources

H. C. Fanshawe (1927) *The History of the Fanshawe Family* – Andrew Reid and Company, Newcastle-Upon-Tyne.

H. C Fanshawe (1907) *The Memoirs of Ann Lady Fanshawe* – John Lane Company.

Denis Le Marchant (1841) *Memoirs of the late Major General Le Marchant 1766-1812* - republished by Spellmount Ltd (1997).

J. Gaspard Le Marchant (1796) *Rules and Regulations for the Sword Exercise of the Cavalry, London.* Printed for the War Office and sold by T. Egerton, Military Library, Whitehall. *https://www.priaulxlibrary.co.uk/articles/article/sword-exercise-cavalry*

Major General John Gaspard Le Marchant (1811 – 1812) *The private letters of Major General Le Marchant addressed to his daughter Katherine Fanshawe (née Le Marchant).* unpublished transcription Fanshawe Collection, Valence House Archives & Local Studies Centre.

Captain T. B. Fanshawe (2016) *Sebastopol to Dagenham : Crimean War letters of Thomas Basil Fanshawe, 33rd (Duke of Wellington's) Regiment* - Valence House Publications *(2016).*

Major T. B. Fanshawe (2018) *Abyssina 1868 : Last Great Expedition of Queen Victoria's Army: The Letters of Major Thomas Basil Fanshawe, 33rd (Duke of Wellington's) Regiment* - Valence House Publications.

Michael Boyes (2005) *A Victorian Rector and Nine Old Maids – 100 years of Cotswold village life - Phillimore & Co Ltd.*

Michael Boyes (2006) *Dying for Glory – The Adventurous Lives of Five Cotswold Brothers Phillimore & Co Ltd., (2006).*

Helen Denison (née Fanshawe) (1844 - 1845) *The letters of Helen Denison (née Fanshawe)* original letters – in the process of transcription Fanshawe Collection, Valence House Archives & Local Studies Centre.

The Fanshawe Collection at Valence House Archives & Local Studies Centre holds an extensive collection of books, documents and papers relating to the many branches of the Fanshawe family. The link below allows access to a brief guide to the collection which expands continually either by purchase of new or used publications as well as by family donations.

http://valencehousecollections.co.uk/wp-content/uploads/ALSguide15_FanshaweLibrary.pdf

Index

In the London Borough of Barking & Dagenham, the Archives & Local Studies Centre at Valence House Museum provides the inspiration for many local heritage projects. Volunteers are encouraged to develop and expand topics of significant local historical interest with the generous support of the professional staff.

In 2016, a volunteer led Heritage Lottery Project researched and published the Crimean War letters of Thomas Basil Fanshawe and from its legacy we now publish the final collection of the letters based on his service in Colonial India during 1875-1877.

The transcriber and editor wish to thank their fellow volunteers and Valence House staff for the interest shown in this research and Karen Rushton is especially thanked, for final proofreading.

Scott Flaving of DWR Trustees continues to offer regimental resources and friendly supportive advice and is always an invaluable help.

We remain always in the debt of John Gordon, thanking him for his trust in granting us the freedom to interpret his fascinating Fanshawe family papers, and his pleasure in our efforts is rich reward.